What Others Are Saying About Moving Messages...

"Rick Bundschuh won't leave good enough alone. That's because he says out loud what most of us know deep down inside: It's *not* good enough. It's not good enough when people come to your church week after week and leave unwelcomed, untouched, and unchanged. It's not good enough when people sit through the sermon and after lunch can't remember what the point was. So whether you're the person up front crafting Sunday morning messages, an elder who wants the church to be the best it can be, or a 20-something headed toward ministry, you need to read this book. It's about how to craft life-changing Sunday morning experiences. It's bold and unconventional—just what the church in the U.S. needs right now."

—John Hambrick
Pastoral Staff, Buckhead Church, Atlanta, and author of
Move Toward the Mess

"Wait. A book about preaching that's actually fun to read and thoroughly engaging, in *addition* to being chock-full of fantastic, disruptive ideas? Bundschuh actually models what he's proposing we consider. And if you care about connecting 21st century church people with the transformative truth of Scripture, you will certainly want to consider this master class on creative preaching."

—Mark Oestreicher
Partner, The Youth Cartel, and author of *Hopecasting: Seeking, Finding and Sharing the Things Unseen*

"Year after year we've attended Kauai Christian Fellowship, where Rick Bundschuh preaches. Sunday after Sunday—through junior high, senior high, college, and now as a young married—our daughter has listened intently to what was happening on the platform. Sundays at KCC are provoking! Rick is a long-range thinker who encourages his congregation to participate in the church journey of affecting the community for Christ, now. For God's sake, read this book and listen for God's nudging. Your congregation will thank you."

—Gary Dixon
Director, Northwest MinCon

"I love Rick Bundschuh's creativity and his passion for teaching the ways of Jesus. He has been a leader and an example for decades, and his message and ideas keep getting better. Read this book. Better yet, use the ideas, and you'll notice a big difference in your teaching."

—Doug Fields
Veteran youth pastor and co-founder,
Downloadyouthministry.com

"Anyone who wants to improve their ability to communicate must read this book. I will be a better speaker because I read it. Rick Bundschuh is one of the most creative people I know. He's lovable, bold, courageous, brilliant, eccentric, a follower of truth, and a communicator extraordinaire. This book contains all the best of Rick and his genius. He brings nuggets of helpful communication to every page. The practical nature of this book mixed with incredible insight into our culture is a breath of fresh air."

—Jim Burns, Ph.D.
President, HomeWord, and author of *Creating an Intimate Marriage* and *Confident Parenting*

"Some communicators talk a good game; others model what they say. Rick Bundschuh is the latter. He knows how to implement change and get us out of a rut. If there were ever a time that the Sunday morning paradigm needs to change, it's now. *Moving Messages* will challenge, frustrate, and maybe even anger you at times, but it will also make you laugh, try new ideas, and empower you to break free from doing things the same old way. Rick is brilliant, funny, and creative. He teaches like Jesus. His book is a gift to us. If you are a communicator of any kind, purchase *Moving Messages* and buy an extra set for your speaker friends. It will revolutionize your teachings."

—Dr. David Olshine
Author and speaker, professor and director of youth ministry, family, and culture at Columbia International University, Columbia, SC

"I love this book! It's witty, fun, and practical—a must-read for today's church leaders. Rick exposes the dangers of sticking with the safe, complacent Sunday morning experience we've all come to expect and leads us into deep waters where pastors work with teams and Sunday mornings are shaped by the unique ways God moves in the lives of his people. It gives us practical ways to communicate timeless truths in fresh and bold ways."

—Danny Ray
Illusionist and author, *Magnificent Mark*

"I hate Rick Bundschuh. For one thing, he lives on Kauai—and I don't. He gets to work with one of the most fun, creative, forward-thinking, and risk-taking churches I've ever seen. I don't. He goes surfing while I have to make do with hiking. He's a talented communicator with the kind of insights that make me wonder why I didn't think of them first. And yet, that's why I loved reading *Moving Messages*—and so will you. His writing style will have you smiling while his ideas and suggestions will have you changing the way you present (or listen to) sermons. This isn't a book for people who are looking for a few tidbits to spice up their messages; it's far more challenging and persuasive than that. This book will have you rethinking how you go about communicating God's truth in a way that changes lives, churches, and communities."

—Ken McCoy

Founder, JumpStart Ministries, Charlotte, NC

MOVING MESSAGES

Ideas That Will Revolutionize the Sunday Experience

RICK BUNDSCHUH

Best-Selling Author of *Soul Surfer*

Group resources really work!

This Group resource incorporates our R.E.A.L. approach to ministry. It reinforces a growing friendship with Jesus, encourages long-term learning, and results in life transformation, because it's:

Relational—Learner-to-learner interaction enhances learning and builds Christian friendships.

Experiential—What learners experience through discussion and action sticks with them up to 9 times longer than what they simply hear or read.

Applicable—The aim of Christian education is to equip learners to be both hearers and doers of God's Word.

Learner-based—Learners understand and retain more when the learning process takes into consideration how they learn best.

MOVING MESSAGES
Ideas That Will Revolutionize the Sunday Experience

Copyright © 2015 Rick Bundschuh

group.com

Credits

Senior Editor: Candace McMahan

Copy Editor: Ann Diaz

Cover Art Director and Interior: Darrin Stoll

All Scripture quotations, unless otherwise indicated, are taken from the Holy Bible, New International Version®, NIV®. Copyright ©1973, 1978, 1984, 2011 by Biblica, Inc.™ Used by permission of Zondervan. All rights reserved worldwide. www.zondervan.com. The "NIV" and "New International Version" are trademarks registered in the United States Patent and Trademark Office by Biblica, Inc.™

Library of Congress Cataloging-in-Publication Data

Bundschuh, Rick, 1951-
  Moving messages : ideas that will revolutionize the Sunday experience / Rick Bundschuh.
  -- First American Paperback [edition].
    pages cm
  ISBN 978-1-4707-3254-7 (pbk. : alk. paper) -- ISBN 978-1-4707-3255-4 (epub) --
  ISBN 978-1-4707-3256-1 (mobi) 1. Preaching. 2. Public worship. I. Title.
  BV4211.3.B86 2016
  251--dc23
                    2015031225

10 9 8 7 6 5 4 3 2 1   24 23 22 21 20 19 18 17 16 15

Printed in the United States of America.

Table of Contents

Introduction

As a pastor, I often feel like an explorer hacking my way through a tangled jungle of tradition, expectations, dogma, and creature comfort. Along the way signs are posted: "Caution! We've Never Gone This Way Before!" "Warning! Liberal Feel-Good Quicksand Ahead!" "Danger! Approaching Career-Ending Minefield!"

Other times I feel like a lonely scout looking for a more effective route to the Promised Land, far removed from the rest of the wagon train that's bumping along a well-trod path.

Sometimes I feel like an inventor, a benevolent Dr. Frankenstein, exalting over some new discovery or clue, all the while tinkering with a monster idea that might just stomp its way onto every pulpit in the world. (And when I find something that really sparks, I catch myself cackling, "Ha, ha, ha! It's alive!")

In my more overcast moods, I think of myself as a pastoral version of Ignaz Semmelweis, a Hungarian doctor who figured out that there was a direct link between a physician's unwashed hands and the spread of disease in his patients. Armed with nothing but statistical proof (microbiology being undiscovered), he made himself such a nuisance to his dismissive peers that he was considered insane and forcibly committed to an asylum, where he died only 14 days later.

In my case, a more likely destination would be the Home for Wacky and Quixotic Pastors.

Explorer, scout, inventor, troublemaker, and perhaps lunatic or martyr—this is my world, the arc of my journey as a pastor, a shepherd to the sheep, and one who wants more than anything to honor the One who gave himself for me.

A Little Background

It was 1972, and I was a young, wet-behind-the-ears pastor to middle school kids in my first real, paying ministry job.

Like everyone else, I tended to teach the way I'd been taught: I studied, came up with a biblical concept, and told the kids about it. I talked, and they listened. It was as simple as that.

I've always maintained that if you can hold the attention of a middle school audience, you can hold the attention of *anyone*, so I worked hard at inserting humor, stories, and illustrations into my talks.

But as catchy as my messages might have been, I still noticed that dull glaze in the eyes of many as they listened politely and I talked at them for much of our time together.

In spite of all the work and effort I put into each study, I sensed that not much was sticking and that, short of lighting myself on fire, most of what took place that morning would not be retained after the kids left the room.

I became desperate for a new pathway but had no idea what to do.

Then I stumbled on the concept of teaching by involvement, an idea that was being championed by groundbreaking educators in secular schools and the International Center for Learning (ICL), a project of Gospel Light Publications.

They called it discovery learning, and it revolved around the simple idea that people learn better when, with a guide and using as many of the senses as possible, they uncover truths by themselves.

From that moment on, I never gave another lecture to my youth group on Sunday morning. Instead, we did all kinds of crazy things: art, skits, drama, creative writing—you name it.

We even got out of the classroom from time to time.

I loaded them in vans and took them to a jail cell where a police captain friend helped me incarcerate them. *Then* we talked about Peter being tossed into the hoosegow. (I so wanted to leave them there for the day, but better judgment and the allure of job security won out.)

We sat in front of crypts in the local cemetery and talked about what it must have been like to watch Lazarus bust out of the grave.

Over the years I took my crew to so many places that I ended up writing a book about these experiences called *On Site*.

We retooled our time together so that kids did the exploring and reporting and applied what they'd learned in the Bible to their own lives. I merely served as their guide.

And it worked. It was never boring (although sometimes kind of weird), and retention went through the roof.

Over the decades I spent in youth ministry, this kind of hands-on, person-to-person, highly sticky kind of teaching was my forte.

Then I became the pastor of a brand-new church.

It was an unexpected and surprising role shift; I'd been launched into the "big time."

Now on Sunday mornings, rather than sneaking kids out of the building to wash the dirtiest car in the parking lot as an experiential lesson in anonymous servanthood, I found myself delivering a 30-minute monologue week after week.

Never wanting to see those glazed-over stares again, I worked hard to make these sermons as engaging as possible while keeping the integrity of biblical truth intact.

At the same time, I watched the information explosion take place.

I noticed the pace quicken. "Get to the point" seemed to be the mantra of the masses.

I remember talking my own teenage kids into watching the classic action movie *Ben-Hur* only to have them moan about how "boring" the film was because all the characters did was "talk." I realized that because of its pacing, this beloved, Oscar-winning flick had lost its ability to connect with modern culture. (So we dismissed the kids, and my wife and I watched the movie by ourselves. We still enjoyed it…and ate the kids' popcorn while we were at it.)

I also sensed that in the midst of the noise bombarding them from every direction, people coming to church were, maybe unknowingly, longing for some kind of human connection, some kind of participation.

The pieces of the puzzle swirled in my head: short attention spans, too much data, a longing for interaction, the goal of high retention.

I became convinced that, in this new era, something had to change on Sunday mornings if I was ever going to be able to say that I had done my best to shepherd the sheep in my care into a life-changing understanding of God's Word.

In the pages ahead, you'll follow the journey I've been on ever since. I hope you'll find something that inspires you, ideas you can use just as they are, and lots of others that you can tweak for use with your own congregation.

My goal is for the principles in this book to become useful tools for you to use to the glory of God. And I would love it if you shot back any ideas of your own that worked well so I can use them myself.

Rick Bundschuh
Kauai, Hawaii
rickbundschuh@mac.com

PART

1

The Journey

The Reason We're Going on This Trip in the First Place

If you've ever driven home from church and drawn a complete blank on the message you've just invested 30 to 45 minutes of your time listening to, here's a bit of good news: You're not alone; your guilty secret is shared by many.

And it may surprise you to know that the experience of coming up empty on your drive home is no longer an occasional event; it's more and more becoming the norm for many churchgoers.

Frankly, most of us don't talk about how little we remember about recent sermons. We figure the problem lies with us, our woefully short attention spans, the woman with too much perfume who distracted us, our lack of education or self-discipline, our spiritual shallowness.

We in the flock are used to long monologues on Sundays, and we're used to not getting a whole lot out of them.

But this is not a blast at those who deliver the goods.

Pastors, we know, have a tough job.

On top of all their other duties, they must crawl up in front of a crowd and do the very thing that tops the list of the most fearful things a human can do: speak to a group.

Not only that; they must be biblically accurate (people are fact-checking), inspiring, humorous, provocative, articulate, engaging, and original each and every week.

If you've never had this monkey on your back, offer to fill a pulpit for a few months and see how *you* like it.

We weigh all of these factors as we grasp for any snippet of sermon content to remember on our Sunday drive home. We wonder why we seem to be more and more uninterested in sitting through another sermon. And we wonder why no one ever complains about a message being too short.

This book is going to annoy and maybe outrage a good number of you. It will likely draw frowns, condemnation, and wagging fingers from a healthy number of laymen and preachers who are sure that anyone who says what I am about to say is obviously riding in the handcart to hell…or if not hell, at least to unvarnished secularism, which is more or less the same.

If Spurgeon is your hero, you're going to hate what's coming. (And just so you know, I've actually read every one of the sermons written by the golden-throated Brit. Just sayin'.)

If you're married to verse-by-verse expository teaching, I might be your poster boy for heresy, my aging carcass tacked up next to *The Message* in the Preacher Hall of Shame.

If you've spent most of your life sitting more or less comfortably in a pew, what I will be promoting will befuddle you because you will most likely say, "If it ain't broke, don't fix it!"

But it *is* broke, or mostly broke.

It doesn't work well anymore and has been losing steam for years.

What is the "it" of which I speak? "It" is the Sunday morning sermon. And, as typically practiced, the Sunday morning sermon is by and large an antique, malfunctioning mode of communication.

Henrietta Mears, the marvelous mid-1900s locomotive of God's energy, is said to have claimed, "The teacher hasn't taught until the student has learned."

Maybe I'm wrong, but I don't think blanking out 30 minutes after a Sunday morning qualifies as learning.

If this is true, the fault sits uncomfortably in the laps of those of us who are responsible for what happens on Sunday morning: pastors, leaders, and, yes, even congregants.

And that's why we're going on this journey.

A Willingness to Explore

I'm a creature of comfort and habit, and I bet you are, too.

I have my morning ritual. The first thing is to put on the kettle and brew up a cup of nasty workingman British tea (a habit I picked up when I attended college in Great Britain). I reach for my favorite mug (it bears an image of Looney Tunes' Marvin the Martian…if you are under 40, just Google him). I then check emails, read a few online news sites, and click on the surf report.

And I like it this way.

Take away my cup of tea and substitute coffee, hot chocolate, or Ovaltine, and my rhythm is destroyed, the universe becomes out of kilter, and the world is suddenly not as it ought be.

And funnily enough, I've never considered that there might be something more enjoyable and satisfying than my little ritual.

My coffee-fiend friends, all now dealers in this "Christian crack" (aka caffeine), try to tell me what I'm missing—and yes, I've heard of hot Dr Pepper—but I don't want to try any of it, thank you very much.

I am simply *not open to change.*

You most likely have some kind of ritual yourself…you probably like it that way as well. And you no doubt feel a little crotchety when someone disturbs that ritual.

In fact, I bet you're just as resistant to change as I am…even when that ritual becomes as tattered, thin, and hole-punctured as that favorite T-shirt we keep reaching for. (Yeah, I have one, too. And yeah, my wife says, "Why do you keep wearing that old rag?" And all I can mumble is "Uh, I dunno. I like it…it's soft.")

We don't like change. It makes us…*uncomfortable.*

Of course this is no big deal when it comes to our morning rituals or comfy T-shirts. But it's a *very* big deal if our resistance to change bleeds into how we communicate the timeless truths of Scripture.

Christianity is disruptive. Our comforts are secondary to the mission at hand. The truth is, done right, Christianity is comforting but rarely comfortable. And if this is true individually, it's also true corporately, in our community of faith, and even in our roles in ministry.

So why am I telling you this by plunking out a book?

Well, I'd like some company. This is an invitation to come along with me on a journey to rethink what we pastors do every Sunday morning. If you're enthralled by the idea, just know that I could use a few more traveling partners. It's been kind of lonely out here.

This is an invitation to come along with me on a journey to rethink what we pastors do every Sunday morning.

I'm inviting you on an expedition into unmapped byways, untraveled roads, and unexplored paths. It could be one of the most helpful and blessed excursions of your pastoral career. It also carries the possibility of painful misfires, cutting criticism, and awkward failure.

In short, to go where I'm going is dangerous.

The journey will disrupt and challenge those comfortable rituals that pastors, leaders, and the whole community of faith have become accustomed to.

The journey will require us to move from the mindset of a maintainer of tradition to that of a pioneer.

It will be fraught with danger, fiascos, and flops.

You'll be lonesome. Few will cheer you on, and many will whisper, "It'll never fly, Orville" in your ear.

You'll have no models to refer to, no studies to hold up, no successes to imitate.

But it will be exhilarating.

The journey has the potential to entirely change the way you communicate on Sunday morning—and to hotwire God's truth for your congregation in such a way that you can sense the sizzle as the Spirit electrifies them.

You may find that conversations get deeper, people start connecting, and the overall faith of your congregation becomes stronger.

And you just may find that those people who have dropped out of fellowship, thinking church is boring or has nothing to offer them, come back.

Preparing for the Road Ahead

A few things are needed to properly prepare for this journey.

First, you must empty your "presumption backpack." Dump the skepticism and the "none of this will work with my congregation" thoughts.

At the same time, unload the idea that you've discovered a new template that will lead your church to new heights and explode it into mega-church territory. Ideas and concepts you will find in these pages; a template you will not. Every community of faith, every leader, and every situation is different.

The ideas in this book are not one-size-fits-all ministry spandex.

They are simply tools. Tools whose use is demonstrated in the pages that follow but not limited to those uses.

What you create with those tools will look wonderfully different than what I might create with the same tools.

What *is* important to bring along on this journey is a spirit of adventure and a willingness to at least consider doing things that are out of the ordinary.

Bring curiosity. Bring wonder. Bring that wide-eyed mischievous spirit that once led you to mix the chemicals you found under the kitchen sink or experiment with the burning power of a magnifying glass.

And yes, you might catch the house on fire.

The Changing and the Unchanging: New Methods, Timeless Truths

I have some acquaintances who are stuck on the King James Version of the Bible. When I say "stuck," I don't mean that they favor it or feel most comfortable using this translation or are so old that they were around when it was translated. I mean "stuck" as in they're convinced that there's *no other* viable and reliable English translation of Scripture.

I find this a tad bit narrow…and nutty.

We all know that language mutates. New words are added to the lexicon; some disappear. (When was the last time you used the word *groak*? It's a delightful word but has been lost for so long lost that even Microsoft Word's spell check doesn't recognize it.) And meanings change. (Does the sentence "Don we now our gay apparel" have the same meaning as when first penned? I rest my case.)

Therefore, for people to understand the Bible, new, fresh translations using current idioms are necessary.

The original Greek and Hebrew of the Bible remain timeless; the words we use in our language to express those thoughts change.

But what if I were to suggest that while the truths of Scripture are timeless, the methods used to convey those truths need constant reevaluation to be effective?

 While the truths of Scripture are timeless, the methods used to convey those truths need constant reevaluation to be effective.

Consider how the *medium* that carries Scripture has changed. From papyrus scrolls to illuminated manuscripts to mass-produced Bibles in leather covers to apps on mobile phones, the vehicle for carrying Scripture has evolved.

And now more Christians carry their Bibles with them constantly than at any other time in history. (Whether they read them more often is a different question.) Call out a passage on Sunday morning and lots of heads lower to scan their screens, not to flip pages. (Or at least we hope that's what they're doing!)

Also, have you noticed that nobody is smuggling Bibles into China anymore? Why? App-bearing phones and computers are ubiquitous. In fact, most of them are made in China. Whole seminary courses are contained in flash drives. The Bible is more widely available in ways we couldn't even have imagined a couple of decades ago.

Same message, different mode of delivery.

So when it comes to what takes place on Sunday morning, and in particular in what we call the sermon or the message, it seems that most of us "sermonators" are stuck in the era of hymnals and slide projectors.

The fear, among pastors as well as many congregants, is that any vehicle other than the conventional sermon will somehow mute, distort, or devalue the message. In other words, the message will be changed by the medium.

The fear is of catering to the masses' unrestrained appetite for amusement and entertainment, thus making what takes place on a Sunday morning as weighty as soap bubbles.

I believe these fears are unfounded.

At least they're unfounded if a community of faith has a deep and immovable commitment to the ancient orthodoxy of the Christian faith and a high view of the Scriptures as the Word of the living God.

This is the foundation upon which all messages and teaching for a viable Christian life is built.

Naturally, if one sees the Christian faith as something that needs to mutate with culture or considers the Bible a book of nice suggestions, whatever comes out on a Sunday morning, regardless of the medium, regardless of how engaging it is, will be laced with spiritual cyanide.

Our job is to understand the culture in which we live and to be alert to the most effective means of delivering the timeless truths of the Bible.

Oh, by the way…to *groak* means to stare at someone silently while they're eating in the hope that they'll share their food. Like what my dog does while I'm having dinner.

I thought you'd like to know.

PART

2

The Case for a
New Paradigm on
Sunday Morning

The Importance of Experiential Worship

Experiential learning. Yeah, I know the term sounds postmodern, college snobbish, with a touch of New Age.

But it actually just means learning something by engaging in more than a passive role.

It's also the shortest route to the kind of learning that actually changes behavior, thinking, and attitudes.

Prove it? Okay, here's an example:

As a kid I hated avocados. I wouldn't touch them. I picked them out of any dish or salad and turned my nose up at any meal that contained the mushy green things.

Oh, did I say that I'd never actually tasted an avocado? I just didn't like the way I imagined it would taste. People told me they were delicious, but I dismissed their comments out of hand.

And then one day, by accident or to impress some avocado-loving girl I had a crush on, I tasted one.

Yum!

The *experience* of tasting an avocado changed everything: my attitude, my thinking, and my dietary behavior.

Every Sunday, we pastors deal with people who have preconceived ideas about God, values, priorities, lifestyles—you name it. To them we offer something new, unfamiliar, and by and large untouched by our culture. We offer the ideas, values, hope, and rhythm of the kingdom of heaven.

Helping people have life-changing and continuing experiences with God is what all pastors worth their salt desire to do every Sunday morning.

The big question is, how well is that working?

We come together for the experience of worship and often measure our effectiveness by how many people attend…which is certainly one indicator, as people usually vote with their feet. But numbers don't give us much of a handle on whether lives are being touched by God.

We come together for community, but in most cases people at church don't talk to anyone but their friends.

We come together for enlightenment, inspiration, and guidance from the Scriptures, but there are few ways to measure what has taken place inside the heart.

With experiential learning, rather than sitting passively during church services, every believer is given opportunities to participate in deep, meaningful ways.

I know this sounds a bit scary to most of us who like things done decently and in order. We fear that the congregation will run amok and chaos will ensue as they all do their own thing.

And I get it. I've witnessed such bedlam in a church service.

I once attended a church in Baja California that encouraged *full participation* during the musical part of the worship service. Everyone was given an instrument of some kind to bang on: shakers, tambourines, claves, washboards, castanets, cabasas, percussion blocks, güiros …you name the noisemaker, someone had it.

Hoo boy!

Did you know that there are some people who can't find the beat of a song…ever? No God-endowed sense of rhythm or timing whatsoever. And did you know that those people should *never* be given a tambourine?

But I do have to admit, it was, in some ways, riotous good fun.

I'm not sure the racket was conducive to helping us draw closer to God, but it *was* full involvement, and it *was* a worship service I'll never forget.

So instead of handing out instruments to everyone in attendance, how can we make the Sunday morning hour an experience people have rather than just an event they attend?

 How can we make the Sunday morning hour an experience people have rather than just an event they attend?

Well, it's an *experience* if something touches them, if the Holy Spirit moves their hearts.

It's an *experience* if they have an aha moment—if illumination comes streaming in, if a new perspective suddenly makes apparent something they hadn't seen before.

It's an *experience* if people are in some way bound to other worshippers.

It's an *experience* if, even for a moment, they see God in a new light, understand an aspect of his nature in a way they'd never before considered, and if even for a flash, God is revealed to them.

It's an *experience* if at the end of the service, something sticks with them: an idea they can't stop turning over in their minds, a realization that leaves them marveling, a new motivation to pursue goodness, a godly stain that doesn't easily wash off.

I don't think there's a pastor in the world who wouldn't hope that his 30-minute contribution to Sunday mornings would result in this kind of experience.

And I think the most humble among us are the ones who would honestly confess we rarely are assured that these experiences are truly taking place under our watch.

One of the greatest mistakes a pastor can make is to assume that presenting divine data guarantees a spiritual experience.

Consider Nicodemus, who, like most of the men in his high position in the Sanhedrin, had deposited the entire Old Testament into his memory bank. But all that data, as good as it was, didn't give him a clue as to what Jesus was getting at when he started talking about being "born anew" (see John 3).

James cautioned believers not to just be sponges of data but to be involved in life-altering, experiential faith: "Don't fool yourself into thinking that you are a listener when you are anything but, letting the Word go in one ear and out the other. *Act* on what you hear! Those who hear and don't act are like those who glance in the mirror, walk away, and two minutes later have no idea who they are, what they look like" (James 1:22, *The Message*).

In our leadership team meetings, we refer to what we are trying to do as "moving the ball down the field."

We do everything we can to create Sunday morning experiences that move the ball down the field toward the goal of transforming each and every person there into the image of Christ.

And we understand that for some people, that movement is measured in inches, not in yards. But for us, it is at least movement in the right direction.

Teaching Like Jesus

Around 2,000 years ago, the hills of Galilee buzzed with excitement over a new rabbi who was teaching in a powerful and gripping way...mostly by way of stories.

Today, religious and secular experts recognize Jesus as a master communicator, yet the methods used in virtually every church on Sunday mornings bear little resemblance to his way of teaching.

I suggest that our wisest course is to carefully consider how Jesus taught and, if possible, to imitate him.

Not a Lot of Bible Quoting

One interesting thing about the teaching of Jesus is how infrequently he quoted Scripture.

As was customary for Jewish boys, Jesus would have memorized the Torah (Genesis, Exodus, Leviticus, Numbers, and Deuteronomy) by the age of 10 and the rest of the Old Testament in the following years (not to mention the fact that, as God incarnate, he actually breathed those Scriptures into existence). Yet in his teaching, Jesus never did a verse-by-verse exposition of an Old Testament book.

And while his allusions to the ancient text were frequent, he actually quoted only a few lines now and then. Yet all of his teachings were in concert with Scripture.

While Jesus ministered to people who were, for the most part, very familiar with Scripture, the apostles often engaged people with no knowledge at all of the Torah or the gospel. And they didn't do any verse-by-verse explorations of Scripture either.

Instead they got the conversational ball rolling by talking about the everyday lives of those they were trying to reach. For example, when Paul talked to the philosophers in Athens, he began by referring to the statues they'd erected all over the city. Before long they began to question him, and ultimately they were engaged in genuine dialogue about his "new teaching" (see Acts 17:16-32).

I'm not suggesting that we eliminate the Bible on Sundays, but I do propose that we use what we need to get the job done... and no more.

Variety

Jesus used an assortment of devices to make his point. No one could claim, "Same place, same thing" about how Jesus delivered his message.

For example, some scholars suggest that, when he delivered them in the original Aramaic, some of Jesus' adages actually rhymed (which makes Jesus a rapper of sorts).

Jesus sometimes used rhetoric, a style of teaching held in esteem by the Romans. He also used the methods of dialogue and argument favored by the Jewish leaders of the day. In reality, he was using styles of teaching that were, for his time, very contemporary.

Humor

There's no doubt that humor was part of Jesus' stock-in-trade, as he used hyperbole, satire, and jesting in his teaching and interaction with others.

Can you sense this in the following? "Which of you, if your son asks for bread, will give him a stone? Or if he asks for a fish, will give him a snake? If you, then, though you are evil, know how to give good gifts to your children, how much more will your Father in heaven give good gifts to those who ask him!" (Matthew 7:9-11).

Stories and Parables

Jesus used stories and parables to help his listeners understand big ideas. And often he didn't tie the stories up with a bow; instead, he forced his listeners to really think, to figure out the meaning themselves.

And these stories weren't fairy tales. Quite frequently they were troublesome or provocative; often they were cautionary tales with tragic endings.

Illustrations and Metaphors

Jesus frequently referred to his surroundings, including common, everyday items and people at hand to make his point.

For example, when he described the consequences of leading a believer astray, he said, "If anyone causes one of these little ones—those who believe in me—to stumble, it would be better for them to have a large millstone hung around their neck and to be drowned in the depths of the sea" (Matthew 18:6). People of his day were very familiar with millstones: enormous stones weighing hundreds of pounds that were used for grinding grain. So the image of a person having one of these stones hung around his neck and then being thrown into the ocean was truly horrifying. Jesus clearly meant for this image to be indelibly imprinted on his listeners' minds.

Today the word *millstone,* in most people's minds, conjures up a picture of…nothing. To make Jesus' meaning clear, then, we should at the very least project an image of a millstone and describe its weight to give our listeners the chilling experience that Jesus intended.

Wherever he went, Jesus used objects at hand to make piercing, unforgettable points. For example, sitting on the edge of a well, he used water to describe the work of the Holy Spirit in the life of a believer, using the natural world to give his listeners a glimpse into the supernatural.

Interaction

Jesus taught through interaction, dialogue, conversations with individuals and groups. He asked a lot of questions—the kind of sticky questions that get people thinking and talking. I'm convinced the disciples' faith took root during talks with Jesus around a campfire.

 [Jesus] asked a lot of questions— the kind of sticky questions that get people thinking and talking.

Interestingly, Jesus rarely taught by delivering long monologues, which is the primary teaching method used in churches today.

Even what's now called the Sermon on the Mount was hardly a sermon but a collection of mini messages.

Just for kicks, time how long it takes to read John 14–16, Jesus' lengthiest recorded monologue. Unless you read it r-e-a-l-l-y s-l-o-w-l-y, you'll find the passage is a lot shorter than a typical sermon.

The Apostle Paul, having been schooled by the Pharisees, might have put people to sleep with his teaching, but Jesus, through his winsome and clever methods of communicating, never did.

And neither should we.

How Ideas Are Absorbed

"What I hear, I forget; what I see, I remember; what I do, I understand." —Chinese proverb

How many commercial messages bombard a person each day? Nobody really knows, not even the marketing folks who *should* know. Guesstimates range from a few hundred to thousands. But one thing we do know: It's a lot.

Fortunately, we manage to slough off most of the commercials bombarding us, except for those that slip into our subconscious minds and urge us to choose Pepsi instead of Coke or Apple instead of PC.

Because it's their business (and an enormous one at that), marketers know a lot about how people absorb and retain ideas.

41

A television ad campaign for Charmin bathroom tissue ran from 1964 to 1985, an incredibly long run for one campaign. It was brilliantly conceived by someone who understood how people absorb and act on messages.

The commercial featured a crotchety grocery store manager named Mr. Whipple.

Apparently this guy had nothing better to do than chase away customers who were so enamored by the softness of the Charmin brand of bathroom tissue that they would take it off the shelves and squeeze it.

In these 30- to 60-second spots, Mr. Whipple would see the violation and come racing down the aisle to liberate the abused TP while scolding the patrons with his mantra, "Please, don't squeeze the Charmin!"

It doesn't get much dumber than this—or more brilliant.

This ridiculous ad led potential customers to actually touch the product. The marketing people knew that once customers touch a product, they're much more likely to purchase it. Another case in point: car dealers who urge us to test-drive the cars we fancy. (To delve into this, I encourage you to read "The Power of Touch" in the August 2008 issue of the journal *Judgment and Decision Making*.)

So what does squeezing toilet paper have to do with anything that might take place in your church on a Sunday morning?

Well, it demonstrates that people retain ideas best when as many senses as possible are involved in the process.

 People retain ideas best when as many senses as possible are involved in the process.

For example, you can tell me how to tie a square knot, and I'll probably look at you with a blank stare.

Hand me a drawing with arrows and dotted lines showing how to tie a square knot, and I'll begin to grasp the concept.

But give me a length of rope, show me how, let me look at the drawing and then practice, and with any luck, I should be able to not only tie a square knot but also remember how.

Suppose I want to communicate what it's like to live a life full of grace.

I could try to explain the concept in theological and biblical terms.

I could explain it using analogies or stories that illustrate the biblical idea.

I could show a film clip illustrating it.

I could walk into the audience and hand out gift cards as an act of grace.

I could walk into the audience and hand out gift cards and ask the recipients to give them to others as a way to show grace.

Clearly, *experiencing* grace is a much more powerful way of understanding the concept than simply being *told* about it. It's the experience that gives us the ability to take an abstract concept and put work boots on it.

We pastors are privileged to communicate the most important, life-changing message the universe contains. Yet we prefer to do it using the least successful method available to us. If God designed people to absorb and retain ideas in a variety of ways, common sense would suggest that we take advantage of all of them.

 We pastors are privileged to communicate the most important, life-changing message the universe contains.

PART

3

Creating an
Environment
for Success

Where Good Things Run Wild

"And the more I considered Christianity, the more I found that while it had established a rule and order, the chief aim of that order was to give room for good things to run wild." —G.K. Chesterton

As a consummate thief of brilliant ideas, I stole the motto for our church community—"Kauai Christian Fellowship...where good things run wild"—from the big man himself, G.K. Chesterton.

I think it sets the perfect tone for things on Sunday mornings to be...uh, um, *unusual.*

I have the freedom to tinker with a long-entrenched style of communicating on Sunday morning only because our team has done a lot of hard work to create an atmosphere in which things that are good are permitted to run amok.

Here are some things about church atmosphere that all church leaders should consider if they hope to start tampering with how they deliver the message on Sunday mornings.

Cast the Church as a Family

There are a lot of biblical metaphors for the church.

Paul described the church as the "bride of Christ," a metaphor that clearly spoke tons to him but frankly doesn't do much for me. (I don't look good in lace.)

Then we have the shepherd and sheep analogy, which sounds kind of inviting unless you have spent any time around actual sheep.

The metaphor of the church as a body works on many levels.

But of all the terms used in the New Testament, I find the word *family* to be the most helpful. Paul used this term in his letter to the church in Thessalonica: "And in fact, you do love all of God's family throughout Macedonia. Yet we urge you, brothers and sisters, to do so more and more" (1 Thessalonians 4:10).

If I'm reading our culture correctly, the idea of the church as an institution, a keeper of tradition, a retreat from the world, a lighthouse of spiritual and moral guidance, or a God-tinged event that people attend doesn't resonate nearly as much as the idea of the church as a family to belong to.

And yes, if the church is a family, there are some pretty dysfunctional ones among us. But there are some pretty healthy ones, too—churches that demonstrate the same kind of behavior that healthy families do.

For example, they...

- **Create a genuinely warm and inviting environment.**

Some homes are sterile and cold, and some make you want to be adopted the moment you walk in.

Some are so disheveled that you politely refuse any food you're offered; others have gone the other way, causing you to wonder if they'll disinfect you before entering. And then there are those that are just plain comfortable.

In some homes, family members offer you a warm cookie within minutes and call you "sweetie" or "sugar" (especially in the South). In others, you may only get a grunt from a family member absorbed in the latest handheld device.

Helping a congregation become a warm and inviting family is vital.

- **Acknowledge that they have weird uncles and aunties.**

Every biological family has them, and so does every church family. Some churches have a lot of them, in fact, and you're probably putting a face and name to at least one of them right now.

They're the peculiar, eccentric, nutty, cranky, difficult people who are, like it or not, part of our family.

And of course, when new people show up and we see old Uncle Oddball making a beeline toward them, we're quick to run interference and sometimes even reprimand improper behavior. Still, we value these strange folks and try to find a useful place for them.

For example, one older member of our church seems to run on cranky juice. But he shows up early every Sunday to help straighten chairs, fold handouts, and do whatever needs to be done.

He also likes to sit in one particular place; in fact, he kind of thinks he owns that spot. Not too long ago, he had to be admonished for grumpily informing a visitor that the seat she had chosen was *his* seat and she would have to find another.

- **Understand that everybody has a purpose and an essential job to do.**

I don't know about you, but I hate going into a house where the parents do all the work while able-bodied teens lie around doing nothing.

In healthy families everyone pitches in, doing what's appropriate for their age, skill set, and maturity. So should it be in the church family.

- **Celebrate everyone.**

Remember when your mom put your lousy attempts at art on the fridge door as if they were the work of Rembrandt? I promise you, she was not overwhelmed by your skill; she was celebrating your effort.

We do that in a family. The success of one of us is the success of all. The pain, grief, or struggle of one is that of all.

Healthy families are always on the verge of a party for someone or something.

> **Healthy families are always on the verge of a party for someone or something.**

So should it be in a church.

Ever had Janitor Sunday? Those who clean the church (whether they're paid or unpaid) are celebrated, thrown a party, and showered with blessings. If not, you should try it. It makes it much easier to get people to help.

- **Hold one another accountable.**

Members of healthy families check up on each other. As a unit, they call out a family member who's misbehaving or tarnishing the family name. They quickly know who's hurting and who needs help.

Healthy church families hold each other accountable as well.

This is easier in small churches; in larger churches it takes more intentionality to ensure that everyone has the opportunity to be in a small group of brothers and sisters who will do life with them.

- **Recognize that sooner or later someone will be disappointed.**
No family is perfect. Sometimes they'll elbow you, most of the time unintentionally but occasionally the jab is well-aimed. From time to time they'll take the last cookie or the biggest slice of pie. Tempers may flare; unkindness may be shown.

If you're in a family, you can count on it happening sooner or later. And when it does, healthy families apologize, forgive, and patch things up.

And through it all—through teenage angst, dumb choices, celebrations, disappointment, loss, trials, and all of the other unpredictable things life throws at us—we stick together.

Because we're a family.

Be Aware of the First Five Minutes

Many believe that people new to a church form a positive or negative impression within the first five minutes.

I don't completely agree. I think it takes some people six or seven minutes.

The point is that what happens initially—ease of parking, the warmth of the people you first encounter, and so on—either heightens or hinders receptivity to the entire Sunday experience.

Because most of us pastors don't get out much on Sundays, we have little idea of what it's like to stumble into a worship service for the first time.

So whenever I travel, I make it a point to attend other churches to see how it feels to be an unknown newcomer.

My experiences have been mixed. In some churches, no matter how long I lingered, I was not approached or welcomed by anyone. In others, I was welcomed only by people who wore badges and were obviously assigned to the job. In a few, virtually everyone I met noticed I was new and greeted me warmly.

In some cases, I could easily locate the restrooms; in others, I had to ask around.

In some cases, I was familiar with nearly every song and could join in worship. In others, every song I heard was new…and I didn't sing because I was afraid I'd hit a wrong note.

And in all of these experiences, I learned that what they say about the first five minutes…is spot on.

Consider the Vibe

Every church community has a vibe, an emotional atmosphere. Generally one can sense it even before entering the door of the meeting room.

Many church environments are corny. Many are sterile.

Some proudly display the trendy look and feel of 30 years ago. (Wait long enough, and blond furniture, fake wood paneling, and shag carpet *will* make a comeback. Maybe even bell-bottoms.)

Some are *too* hip. Churches trying for a modern feel often overdo things with huge numbers of colored lights and tons of stage fog, leading people to think they've wandered into a heavy-metal concert.

In some, you're greeted by guys in suits and ties; in others, they're in jeans and T-shirts. In some, you're not greeted by anyone at all.

In some, the layout is formal, with an altar, pews, and such. In others, you're dwarfed by semicircular rows of chairs and a stage with all kinds of high-tech gadgetry. And in a very few, you walk into a room with dozens of café tables and chairs and a few sofas.

In short, these days when you walk into a church, you might feel like you're in a museum, an event center, or a big Starbucks.

Rethink the Space

What does all of this have to do with delivering memorable messages? After all, there are vibrant Christian communities meeting in jungle huts, open-air cabanas, and warehouses all over the world, so why does it matter?

While it's true that God can and does move, regardless of the look and feel of our physical meeting spaces, doing some hard thinking about those spaces and implementing some changes can make it easier to experiment with new ways of communicating. If you have control over the design and color of your meeting room, consider the subtle emotion or expectation it creates.

I know that most pastors are pretty much stuck with what they've got when it comes to their facilities' shape and size. Even so, a whole lot can be done to create a space that encourages greater community and connectivity.

For example, many older churches are designed as long rectangles, with rows of pews stretching to the back door. And in most of these churches, the pulpit is elevated in the corner of the stage.

This layout, especially an elevated pulpit, puts up psychological barriers between the one in the pulpit and those in the pews. It suggests that the message giver is somehow not like the rest of us sinners; he or she is a few steps closer to heaven.

And the long rectangle prevents interaction among the people in the pews. It requires people to turn around to converse, straining their backs and necks, whereas a curved or clustered seating arrangement requires them only to lean forward.

The long rectangle also diminishes engagement. Everyone knows that the further back you are from the action, the less engaged you're expected to be. That's why the most coveted seats in a typical church are the ones lining the rear, and the ones most likely to remain empty are in the first row.

This used to drive me nuts.

I scratched my head for a long time as I tried to figure out how to get bottoms into those empty seats.

I wondered if doing a guilt trip would work. I considered charging a premier-seat fee for the back rows and paying people to sit up front. Finally it occurred to me that I might be able to beguile the congregation into occupying the best seats in the house.

 I considered charging a premier-seat fee for the back rows and paying people to sit up front.

So we tried an experiment.

We bought sofas. Nice, soft, stylish, comfortable sofas. And without saying a word, we put them up front.

Problem solved.

All peasants, lepers, unwashed youth, and those late to church: Your place is the back row. We have limited first-class seating, and you'd better get to church early to take advantage of it.

It also contributed to the cool vibe we were aiming for.

Here's What Else We Did

Our team intentionally tried to make our meeting room feel like a huge Starbucks. We copied their color scheme (I'll have a tall latte and a color chip, please). And every Sunday we invite folks to bring the coffee they pick up from our barista into the meeting room. (Yes, we blew bucks on a first-class coffee setup.)

And if we weren't currently at maximum capacity each Sunday, I can tell you what else we'd do: We'd replace chairs in rows with small, round café tables and chairs. Gathering around a table invites community and discussion far more than sitting in rows of pews or immovable chairs.

Why Starbucks? Well, it's familiar, has a masculine edge (as opposed to, say, "La Petite Tea Shoppe and Nail Emporium"), and most important, it's a comfortable, disarming place that invites conversation.

Starbucks is more than a coffee shop; it's a gathering place. Unlike fast food places, where furnishings are designed to be so uncomfortable you want to eat and go, Starbucks is designed to encourage you to linger, have another cup of coffee, go online, meet someone, make a friend.

Which is what I want to happen when our church tribe gathers on Sundays.

We also have friendly roamers (kind of like greeters but without the silly badges) who meet and greet folks as they sit down or as they come into the foyer and even the parking lot. (Most of our regulars show up just as things start rolling, so our friendly roamers are greeting mostly newcomers.)

Instead of a stage, we built a riser that extends into the congregation.

We also pay a lot of attention to signage, parking, centralized information zones, sound, projection, and even the distance from one trash can to another.

All these details are designed to create an atmosphere that supports our objectives before the morning even starts. Each element subtly communicates what to expect. And each element makes it easier for me to launch messages that deviate from the lecture format most churchgoers expect.

What Could *You* Do?

If your church has a long, narrow layout and an elevated pulpit, you could certainly get out of the loft and move closer to the people. You could also turn the center of the room sideways, reorienting the seating from long and narrow to a wide, clamshell arrangement. You could add café tables or sofas.

It could cost money.

It could mean getting rid of some of those sacred cows such as the massive hand-carved podium made by somebody's great grandfather.

It could mean offending the flower ladies by letting them know that the meeting room will no longer be decorated like a funeral hall.

And it could give you a quiet advantage as you help the congregation become more receptive to change.

Get Technology Right

The technology train that has been roaring through our culture has not left the average church unaffected. Video projection units adorn most churches, pew Bibles and hymnals remain mostly untouched (if they remain at all), and even tiny congregations have launched websites.

Technology offers an incredible array of tools that can help make every message compelling and memorable.

 Technology offers an incredible array of tools that can help make every message compelling and memorable.

But these tools must be used properly.

For example, suppose you're including a video story in your message. Nothing negates the power of a great video like a fumbling operator at the helm of the computer. You've no doubt suffered through something like this: The image comes on, but the sound doesn't, or the sound is overlaid by another program playing music, and so on.

And the moment, which could have been so powerful, is lost.

Simple things, such as mistimed song lyrics or a washed-out screen from too much light, subtract from the number of tools that can be used to build a message with something other than one person's voice.

So it's vital to get the right technology and capable people who are trained to operate it.

Leave the Stage

In normal church settings, the pastor teaches from a spot on the platform while the people sit safely in their pews or chairs, observing and listening.

I would like to suggest that you leave the stage from time to time, walk in the audience, distribute things, touch shoulders, sit next to someone as you explain an idea.

If you aren't in the habit of doing this, it will shock the congregation. They'll stiffen as you approach.

But something else will happen. Things will get real, people will pay attention, and they'll engage.

Lose the Same Place, Same Thing

Every church has a liturgy, even non-liturgical churches. Four songs, announcements, a sermon followed by a closing song—this is a liturgy of sorts.

While some people may enjoy the predictability of a service that never changes, the normal order of things may not best serve the big idea you want to get across on a given Sunday. For example, a message on praise might be better presented by punctuating the teaching with songs of praise. So that morning the "liturgy" would look like this: a song followed by a short teaching, followed by a song, a teaching, a song, the offering, a teaching, another song, a final teaching, and a fifth song.

In other words, the elements of the service are arranged to accentuate the big idea of the morning.

This means that the order of service may vary from week to week in some way or another.

And that ain't bad...just different.

Consider the Men

It's no great secret that going to church services isn't on guys' top-10 list of stuff they want to do. In fact, the average male tends to be suspicious of the church experience, figuring that it's emotional, touchy-feely, and out of sync with the world he lives in.

Re-engineering the morning so that it resonates with men as well as with women is both wise and essential if you truly want to revolutionize the Sunday experience.

The things that click with men are often subtle and not too difficult to achieve. Here are a few examples:

- Sing worship songs in a key that men can sing.

- Don't ask people to hold hands or hug their neighbors. Yes, there are some huggers in every crowd, but 8 out of 10 men cringe at the thought of touching people they don't know.

- Create a visual environment men are comfortable with. Ditch the flowers. Scrap the doilies. You don't have to transform the church into a lodge with moose heads mounted on the walls (although I think that would be pretty cool); just design the interior of your meeting room with men in mind.

- Keep it short. Why go for 30 minutes if you can say it in 20?

- Keep it relevant and practical. Men strongly respond to ideas that have handles on them, that challenge them to *do* something. Women, on the other hand, tend to respond to concepts that help them *feel* something...which is why 99 percent of puppy pictures posted on Facebook are posted by women.

- Provide them with *good* coffee. 'Nuff said.

By the way, ensuring that men are attracted to and involved in church has a powerful byproduct. Studies have shown that when men attend church regularly, the likelihood that their children will go to church when they become adults increases dramatically, even if these grown children's spouses don't attend. On the other hand, no matter how devout mothers are, it's unlikely that their children will attend church as adults if their fathers aren't involved.

Teach as a Team

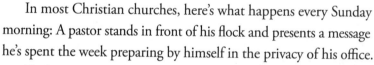

In most Christian churches, here's what happens every Sunday morning: A pastor stands in front of his flock and presents a message he's spent the week preparing by himself in the privacy of his office.

To that pastor, mounting the pulpit to deliver the Word is the center point of the week, the thing that proves he has earned his salary, the high point of his awesome and terrifying responsibility to feed his flock.

From that pulpit he delivers truth, casts vision, inspires, rebukes, encourages, and enlightens.

Many pastors guard the pulpit like a pit bull. They reluctantly give it up when they're on vacation, and unless some grand pooh-bah of Christianity is visiting, they make sure that nobody but themselves gets to deliver the goods on Sunday morning.

Although this is standard practice in most churches, I've been uncomfortable with it for a long, long time. Here's why:

First, it places all the burden of Sunday morning teaching on one person—a burden that only a small percentage of teachers can carry with excellence week after week for years.

If that person is one of those rare, highly skilled communicators, it makes him the crown prince of his domain, the unspoken reason people come to church. And in the worst cases, it makes him a star in his own mind.

This is all dangerous ground. It sets good people up for failure either because they don't have the wherewithal to deliver knockout messages week after week or because they become the lynchpin of the church...and they know it. It also opens them up to the corrupting world of power and control.

The More Chefs, the Tastier the Fare

What if we released our lock grip on the pulpit and allowed others—people with something to say and the ability to say it—to take our place?

Having only one chef cook up the Sunday fare means that other equally talented or even more talented chefs or short-order cooks in the congregation never get to whip up their offerings. And both the congregation and the unutilized chefs are robbed of a blessing. Different voices bring different vantage points, emphases, style, and humor, expanding the menu for all.

What if we took this idea a step further? What if we were to team-teach or teach in concert with others on Sunday morning?

The solo teacher would learn to craft his message as part of a team of spiritual chefs. One week he would deliver the appetizer while someone else delivered the main course and someone else the dessert, only to switch roles the following week.

Yummy!

Message preparation at my church is *no longer a solo act*. It takes a team and collaborative preparation to make it work. I'll take you through a more detailed description in Part 5, but for now, here's a glimpse into how the week unfolds…

The team I work with usually consists of our worship leader, our storyteller, and myself.

At our first meeting, I outline the premise of the message, key ideas, and responses I'm hoping for. At this point, the plan is as solid as Jell-O. As we delve into it, I usually realize that some of my ideas need to be strengthened, some need to be hit from another angle, and some need to be jettisoned altogether.

We also kick around ideas for various vehicles we might use to carry the ideas. We look for methods that we know will be effective and accessible and will allow for interaction—all with the goal of making the message memorable. And of course the methods have to be doable. Many great ideas have been quietly set aside after we've realized we didn't have the talent, time, or budget to make them work.

After a few cups of coffee and numerous sheets of crumpled notepaper, a plan for Sunday morning emerges. By the end of the first meeting, we've outlined how the morning will flow, and that flow may look nothing like the previous Sunday. In other words, the flow every Sunday is dictated by our objective, not by a set model.

While this may seem like a lot of work, it's actually much easier to craft a message as a team than to work in solitude. Bouncing ideas off of others helps me see where I need more focus, and the puzzled looks around the table tell me when I've gone down a rabbit hole.

 It's actually much easier to craft a message as a team than to work in solitude.

Let Others Bring Something to the Table

Here's a fascinating passage of Scripture: "What then shall we say, brothers and sisters? When you come together, each of you has a hymn, or a word of instruction, a revelation, a tongue or an interpretation. Everything must be done so that the church may be built up" (1 Corinthians 14:26).

In this passage, the Apostle Paul describes an example of what took place when the early church gathered, and, my goodness, it sure sounds more like an ensemble performance than a solo act to me.

Over the centuries more than a few churches have experimented with this unscripted way to gather as the body of Christ, but few have held to this format. Even so, there's something here that I believe we should be open to: letting the laity contribute to the

Sunday morning experience, adhering also to Paul's words at the end of the chapter: "Everything should be done in a fitting and orderly way" (1 Corinthians 14:40).

I completely understand the need to ensure that these kinds of offerings are appropriate, of high quality, and biblically accurate. And perhaps the sticky job of having to gently turn down a less-than-inspired idea is enough to avoid opening Sunday morning to congregational input altogether.

But consider the upside of inviting members of the church body to contribute their talents and experiences.

What if someone wrote an especially fine piece of poetry, a worship song without music? Could it be shared? With enough notice, might the poem be put to music by the worship leader and taught to the congregation?

Could someone with a profound thought or powerful experience share it with the congregation, either live, on video, or in a written commentary inserted in the bulletin?

Could a church make space in its foyer for a photographer to display photos celebrating God's creation?

A few months ago we had an event for young teens called Rock U. The point of the weekend was to help kids who wanted to play in a band get to know their instruments and improve their skills. During the song-crafting session, a group of middle school kids, with help from our worship leader, created a short worship song. And we included it in our Sunday morning service, giving credit where credit was due. The experience left a powerful imprint on everyone, especially the students.

The Most Important New Hire: A Storyteller

With the baby boom that following World War II, churches found their nurseries swamped with little tikes, but they didn't give much thought to the game-changing effects on the culture and the church when thumb-sucking toddlers became a massive group of surly teenagers.

Churches, which had gotten along fine for centuries by generally ignoring teens or having a few adult volunteers ride herd on this mostly complacent age group, suddenly began the search for people who could relate to kids and a culture in revolution. They created a new position called youth pastor, and this position was the hot hire of the late '60s and most of the '70s. Every church had to have one, even if it didn't know why.

As these teens grew into adulthood, they sparked what came to be called the worship wars. Younger members of congregations simply didn't engage with traditional church music, which was characterized by choirs, hymnals, and pipe organs. Pastors began to notice that the churches that were experiencing significant growth had ditched the piano and organ in favor of guitars, bass, and—heaven forbid—drums.

They replaced hymnals with overhead projectors so that new rock-tinged songs (often replete with misspellings and poor kerning) could be projected for all to see.

As the worship wars heated up in the '90s, the hottest hire became a gifted worship leader, typically a young man with a guitar strapped around his torso. Choir directors found themselves unemployable.

These changes caught seminaries and Christian colleges largely unaware. They offered no training, specialty focus, or any other kind of guidance for these new hires. It was a time of pioneers, innovators, and creative thinkers, even though the changes they wrought are now part of the status quo.

So what's next?

Well, as in the past, you won't find this new pastoral position listed in college catalogs or in most church budgets, but it's as necessary now as the positions of youth pastor and worship leader. The new position is *storyteller*.

Of course in the end, storyteller may not be the official title. The position might end up being labeled pastor of ministry communications or visual arts pastor or something else.

Regardless of their official titles, what these people *will* do is tell stories.

They'll create or manage the creation of short (two- to four-minute) videos that tell stories of what God has done or is doing in the congregation.

These stories might be what used to be called testimonies, but they'll be trimmed down, edited, and made visually and audibly compelling. The stories may be used as teaching moments, as ways of illustrating theological concepts such as grace. They may be reports from outside the walls of the church: a glimpse into a teen service project, a ministry to the elderly, or some other ministry or event. They may be a vehicle for celebrating something or someone in the congregation.

But regardless of their specific purpose, they'll all be short, professional, and compelling.

And part of the storyteller's job will be to make sure that these stories will be *everywhere*: Facebook, Vine, Instagram, websites… anywhere social media lurk.

Good stories will be shared again and again, gaining a larger life and audience than the ones they were originally created for. Some will be used on Sunday morning, some in home groups, and some only in cyberspace.

Pastors and other church leaders will find themselves creating mini-bite messages that will float out in a variety of forms but will actually, in total, reach far more than a traditional Sunday morning sermon.

It will be the job of the storyteller to capture, edit, and deliver all of these stories.

Where We Tell Our Stories and Why It's Important

At first, God's stories were told around campfires, orally passed on from one generation to another. Even when those stories found their way to paper, Bibles and books were beyond the economic reach of average people, who still learned most of what they knew about God's stories from storytellers and only occasionally in church.

In medieval times, when the Bible was typically delivered in Latin to people who didn't understand that language, the churchgoer would hear God's stories via feast days, pageants, and stained glass images. They were stories told by the media of the day: drama, pageantry, and art.

Once the printing press made the written word accessible to the masses and the public became literate, God's stories found their way into the hands of common people via the King James Bible, tracts, serials, and books.

Our storytellers were primarily preachers, lecturers, poets, and authors.

In the early 1900s, the medium of film became a new vehicle for storytelling. People (except devout Christians) flocked to theaters to watch stories in scratchy black and white flicker on screens.

Unfortunately, the Christian community missed the boat entirely on this powerful story-weaving tool because of a fear of anything having to do with a theater, thus handing the telling of God's stories in this commanding new medium over to Hollywood. And typically, we Christians have been complaining about the perverse stories coming out of "La-La Land" ever since.

But...if you wanted to hear God's stories, church was your primary option, and as long as most people went to church regularly, the stories were told. And sometimes told very well.

Because of strong church attendance, some level of spiritual awareness existed in our culture. People might still behave badly, but at least they acknowledged they were behaving badly, and most had at least a faint imprint of God's Word on them. The stories they heard in Sunday school served as behavioral boundary markers and offered a path back home when they became spiritually lost.

Fast-forward to now. Fewer and fewer people go to church. Most people are largely ignorant of God's real story. And there isn't a trace of a biblical imprint to help guide their understanding or behavior.

Without God's story, the culture drifts and mutates, and people worship just about anything except the Creator of all.

Without God's story, we don't know who we are or what we are capable of in terms of evil or good. We create our own narrative with man as the central character—a story that always ends as a tragedy.

By all measures, it's a dark time. And as often happens in dark times, God provides a way.

That way is technology.

Technology

You might recognize the term *dial-up*. If so, you no doubt feel old already. (For those who came of computer age after 1998, dial-up was a long and annoying way of logging on to the Internet highway.)

You might even have a faint memory of dial phones, which of course were used to call friends to attend witch burnings or displays of alchemy.

Most of us have witnessed the imploding of the record industry, and some of us watched as the Kodak film company exploded into bits and bytes. We're currently experiencing turmoil in the publishing world and observing the collapse of Hollywood as we know it (shh, don't tell them; let it be a surprise). All of this is driven by technological advancements that place powerful tools of creativity into the hands of the average person at a fraction of the previous cost.

It seems clear that those who have the world's most compelling story to tell should be moving quickly to take advantage of this monumental opportunity.

For a modest sum, a church can equip a storyteller with a digital movie camera, an effects-packed computer, and other movie-making equipment. The only thing money can't buy cheaply is creativity.

And creativity is one of those things that God seems to be in charge of.

How to Find a Storyteller

Because it's so new, the storyteller position in a church context is uncharted territory. It's a job that few think exists or will exist. It's a job that few boards and congregations think necessary. And it's a position that few colleges are training their students to fill.

It's a position most churches need right now, but they don't know it.

 Storyteller…a position most churches need right now, but they don't know it.

It's a position that will be filled mostly by young adults, probably film students or those who have been making short media presentations for years on their cell phones, cameras, and GoPros.

These storytellers will primarily be digital natives, those who know their way around the world of social media and are in tune with whatever the next new pipeline for disseminating information is. (I must say, though, I've found that it's presumptuous to discount older generations. There are some quick learners among them who have fully embraced new technologies and offer an amazing depth of creativity and storytelling acumen.)

There are a few easy ways to locate the pool where this talent foams and froths. One, of course, is to check out colleges with strong film programs, such as Biola University and Azusa Pacific.

Nabbing a young person right out of college, setting him or her up with great tools, a creative canvas, and a fair salary would be a terrific win-win for both the church and the graduate.

Another place to look is among the congregation. Poke around to find out who's making films. Check out their work on YouTube; see if they have the chops needed to tell a story with excellence. (As in any creative field, you'll find some who think they have more talent than God or experience has given them, and others who are obvious gems in the rough.)

Entice them with gear purchased by the church: a green screen, lighting, sliders, a drone, nifty software, and lots of stand-alone hard drives or a really big cloud account.

How It Works

The key to making this position pay off is teamwork. A storyteller cannot work in a vacuum.

If part of the storyteller's job is to post videos, photos, and other information on church websites, the various ministries in the church must be proactive about sending the data, art, or images that are needed to tell the story. If the high school pastor lags in getting information to the storyteller about the great things happening in that ministry, that creates a hole in the narrative of the church. Stories that should be told are left untold.

The storyteller position probably affects those doing the teaching more than anyone else.

In past days, the "sermonator" would sequester himself and weave verbal magic through private study, meditation, and sometimes theft…I mean "borrowing."

Now the teacher and the storyteller, as well as the worship leader and maybe others, form a creative team. The teacher may set the message's direction and zero in on its central concept, but the job of identifying the best vehicles for delivering the concept will be shared with others.

Together this team will hammer out the timing of a segment of teaching, a video, a skit, peer-to-peer interaction, and so on. The goal is to ensure that all of the elements work together smoothly and cohesively to make the point.

The storyteller might be asked to find or create a video segment that introduces the morning's theme, illustrates a concept, or cements an application. It may be an open-ended story or parable that requires the congregation to dialogue with each other to derive a conclusion or meaning.

And it will be different from week to week.

Here's an example. One Christmas Eve I wanted to tell the true story of Saint Nicholas. I could have told the story myself, but we decided to go all out and tell the story via video, using custom art, music, and animation that our storyteller created. The result was a thousand times more powerful than it would have been if I'd merely related it. You can see for yourself here: worshiphousemedia.com/mini-movies/48657/the-real-story-of-st-nick.

Now's the Time

The position of storyteller is one of the most exciting and powerful ministry positions to emerge from the technological revolution. It gives those with a story to tell the means by which to tell it and the platforms by which to deliver it.

And who has a better story to tell than people with the aroma of redemption all over them?

The world is constantly using video and other media to tell its story. Now's the time for Christians to grab these tools to tell *his* story!

PART

4

Elements of
Experiential
Teaching

Ingredients of Memorable Messages

Think of all the elements and ideas I'm about to describe as possible ingredients in recipes for truly memorable Sunday morning messages.

Unless you're concocting a stew, you won't use all the ingredients on any given Sunday; instead, you might use two or three one week and a couple of entirely different ones the following week. It all depends on which work best to support the big idea you have in mind.

Teaching in Bits and Pieces

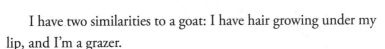

I have two similarities to a goat: I have hair growing under my lip, and I'm a grazer.

I would rather munch on something here and there throughout the day than sit down to a big meal. For me, a three-course dinner is food overload! I prefer to consume food in bits and pieces.

I'm like that with information, too.

Perhaps I have the attention span of a goat as well; within 10 or 15 minutes, my mind checks out and ventures off to points unknown. And that's when I'm *trying* to listen.

I do realize that some people are able to sit quietly and drink in a 30- to 50-minute block of information. But these people are becoming as rare as hair on a billiard ball. For those not born with short attention spans, our culture is in the process of forming this trait into them.

Note the rapid pace of movies. Observe the myriad messages littering the screen as you watch the nightly news. Read blogs.

Brevity rules.

Of course this wasn't always the case.

Consider the first speaker at the dedication of the Gettysburg cemetery in 1863. No, it was not Abraham Lincoln. He was the *second* presenter at this event.

The first speaker was Edward Everett. Although he was or had been the governor of Massachusetts, a congressman, the president of Harvard, a minister to the Court of St. James, the secretary of state, and a senator, Everett was best known as an orator. So he set out to leave his mark on this important occasion by speaking for nearly two hours to a crowd shivering in the November cold.

The second speaker spoke for about three minutes. And the crowd was exceedingly disappointed. Obviously people had a knack for absorbing long-winded oration in those times.

It was only when Lincoln's speech was *published* that it was greeted by universal acclaim.

Interestingly, in today's culture, Lincoln's Gettysburg Address might be considered tediously long.

In American churches we typically deliver the goods in 30- to 45-minute blocks (although in some churches, you might as well throw away your watch).

We pastors tell ourselves that our congregations will starve spiritually if we don't unload the whole dump truck of ideas we've gathered. And since most people sit passively, sometimes nodding their heads, we assume that this big info dump is working out just fine.

But frankly, we're kidding ourselves. Not only is culture moving us all toward shorter attention spans, God's design for how people learn works against the 30-minute monologue.

So one important element of experiential teaching is breaking up the teaching into bits and pieces.

 One important element of experiential teaching is breaking up the teaching into bits and pieces.

This can be done in a number of ways:

TED Talk Style—As you probably know, the longest TED Talk is limited to 18 minutes. Some are 12 minutes; some are 8. Why not break your sermon up like this, punctuating it with worship music, peer-to-peer discussion, or video?

One Message, Many Voices—What if the person who normally delivers the message only gave a portion of it? What if Sunday morning became more of a tag-team event, with different voices and vantage points weighing in on the big idea of the morning? These voices could be live or recorded. Or they could be part of a panel discussion.

Wait for It—What if the last segment of the message was waiting online instead of delivered from the front? (Yes, you'll need to employ the "drop the other shoe" technique to make people *want* to find out the end of the story.)

I've been experimenting quite a bit with teaching in bits and pieces.

We began slowly with a tag-team series on Scriptures that are written as couplets, such as the Lord's Prayer, the Sermon on the Mount, Psalms, and Proverbs. As each message evolved, the other presenters and I compared notes to make sure the pieces fit.

The response of the congregation has been wonderful. They comment frequently that they enjoy hearing more than one voice and style.

The key idea for teaching in bits and pieces is that *the concept is king*. The point is not to fill a given amount of time. (Again, why say it in 40 minutes if it could be said more eloquently and powerfully in 10?) It's not to provide information; we have Wikipedia for that. It's not to show off the preacher's oratory skills or to demonstrate that he studied all week and has thus earned his paycheck.

It's to share a divine idea that can transform lives.

And, yes, this approach does monkey with things like when to take the offering, how to get the musicians back on stage after only five minutes, and when to make announcements. But these are not insurmountable problems compared to the opportunity to really connect the congregation with the message.

By the way, if you decide to teach in bits and pieces, and especially if you share the platform with other teachers, get a stage clock. Only the speaker sees the clock, and it shows how much time he or she has to complete that section of the talk.

I think you know the reason for this: Some folks just talk until they run outta steam. If you're following them, either you'll have to edit on the fly or church time will be extended, which makes no one happy.

The Power of Story

Stories are one of the most potent vehicles for making the abstract concrete, for moving an idea from the head to the heart, for changing how people actually live.

A good story captures our attention and keeps us riveted.

A good story can inspire, warm hearts, impart hope, and free tightly capped emotions.

A good story can also serve as a cautionary tale, the flashing lights that prevent a train wreck.

A good story is almost impossible to resist.

And did I mention that the hallmark of the Master's teaching was storytelling? "He taught by using stories, many stories" (Mark 4:2, *The Message*).

Skilled communicators in or out of the pulpit have long tapped the power of story. And of all the elements of a new paradigm for delivering the goods on Sunday mornings, storytelling is the easiest one to sell.

But where do these stories come from, and should the chief sermonator always be the one to tell them?

 Stories are one of the most potent vehicles for making the abstract concrete, for changing how people actually live.

Of course the big story is about Jesus, and all the narratives and incidents recorded in Scripture point to him. It's important to hone the skill of retelling those stories in fresh, gripping ways.

But there are also new stories to tell...stories that belong to the people sitting among us on Sunday mornings...undiscovered stories that can be powerful, inspiring, and hopeful as well as difficult and tragic. These are the stories of God's interactions with his people now, and they're just as much a part of his story as the ones recorded thousands of years ago.

For example, one morning our teaching consisted of the background stories behind the worship songs we sang. Did you know that Brenton Brown's popular song "Everlasting God" was written at a point in his life when he was in utter despair? Neither did our congregation.

Telling the story of the unimaginable loss that led Horatio Spafford to write "It Is Well With My Soul" introduced an element to worship that morning that would never have been there otherwise.

Stories abound. And it's stories—not principles—that people talk about on their drive home from church.

Stories From the Red Chair

We bought a red leather chair. It's where people are encouraged to tell their stories.

These short (four minutes or less) glimpses into the lives of our own people are used either on a Sunday morning to support the big idea of the message or as an item of interest on social media, or both.

And because these are the stories of people in our church family, they possess an authenticity and encouragement that sometimes outweigh the actual depth of the narratives.

We've found that, in addition to supporting the big idea we're trying to get across on a given Sunday, these stories bind the congregation more closely together. Watching people they've seen around church share personal stories deepens their understanding and affection for one another.

We call these interviews Stories From the Red Chair.

Here's one:

Bob Hammerquist is in his 90s and usually sits in the back of the church wearing headsets we provide for the hearing impaired.

Most people, especially youth, walked past Bob every Sunday without ever thinking of sitting down to talk with him, especially since they had to shout to make themselves heard. But I did, and the snippet that I heard made me want to get his story on film.

It turned out that, as a young lieutenant toward the end of World War II, Bob parachuted into Nazi Germany. His job was to secure a large bridge over the Rhine so that Gen. Patton's tanks could advance into Germany.

In what's now referred to as Operation Varsity, British and Canadian troops were dropped into Germany. A number of transport planes were shot down by anti-aircraft guns, and Bob's division was split up in the confusion. Gathering all the men he could, the young lieutenant, who was getting his first taste of combat, started off for the objective.

He found that the Germans had loaded the bridge with explosives that would be detonated as soon as passage was attempted.

Lt. Hammerquist ordered his men to direct fire across the river at anything that looked like it might house a German soldier while he, armed only with a wire cutter, ran onto the bridge and attempted to snip wires connected to the explosive charges.

As bullets flew by his head and pinged off steel girders, Bob methodically moved along the bridge, snipping wire after wire, fully expecting to be blown sky high at any second.

When he reached the far side of the bridge, a small bridge attached to the larger one blew up, knocking him off his feet and throwing him backward.

In the smoke and debris, he struggled to get up and then continued cutting wires on the other side of the bridge, working back toward his men, who were still firing furiously to prevent the enemy from getting a good aim at their brave officer.

Finally a round hit Bob in the back, bowling him down, but he clambered to his feet and finished his task before throwing himself into the safety of the sandbagged area where he'd started.

Apparently he had done his work well, for the main bridge didn't blow up. Soon Patton's tanks arrived and crossed into Germany.

While Bob was recuperating in the hospital, he found that he'd been awarded the Distinguished Service Cross, the second-highest military award that can be given to a member of the U.S. Army. (His men thought he got gypped and that he actually deserved the Medal of Honor.)

After Bob told his story, the room erupted in a standing ovation. Now virtually everyone goes out of their way to acknowledge him, and he's a celebrity among the younger set.

Excavate for the stories in your congregation. You might be surprised what you find. In our relatively small community, we have an Olympic volleyball player, a war hero, one of the original creators of the Ironman Triathlon, a child movie star, a plane crash survivor, and a host of other interesting people with sometimes mind-blowing stories that dovetail nicely into the messages of grace we craft.

Everyone has a compelling story to tell; they just don't always realize it. As you go about life, listen for stories. When you hear a good one, make notes and drop them in a story file. How you might actually use the story may not be obvious at the time, but the fact that it's a good story is enough to save it. My file of interesting stories really gives me a head start when I'm looking for ways to illustrate an idea.

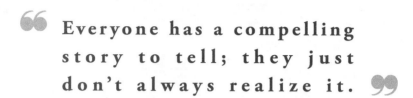

Everyone has a compelling story to tell; they just don't always realize it.

Whether they're told around a campfire, spun from a stool on a stage, or told via a YouTube video, the power of stories transcends the ages.

How to Conduct a Good Interview

Three people are needed for each Story From the Red Chair: the filmmaker/editor, a person skilled at asking good questions, and a live human to sit in the chair.

Plopping someone down in front of a camera is no guarantee that you'll get a good story. The person conducting the interview is the key to drawing out the subject and making sure the story you're after is told in a compelling, honest way.

Here are a few tips:

Before filming, conduct a pre-interview. Listen to the person's story, and identify the part you want to focus on. Then create a list of questions that will get to the heart of the matter.

For example, a man in our church survived a commercial airplane crash. We needed to know the context in order to get to the heart of the story, so we asked him to describe what happened. (A commuter flight ran out of fuel…really. The pilot did a nosedive and then flattened out over a forest, allowing the plane to fall through the trees as branches slowed the descent. Everyone survived with only minor injuries.)

For our purposes, these facts weren't the most important part of the story, so we followed up with these questions:

- Has this event affected your willingness to fly or your trust in the aviation industry?

- The fact that you all lived and most of you simply walked away is attributable either to luck or a miracle. How do you see it?

- What goes through your mind when you think you're going to die?

- How has this experience affected how you view life?

- How has this experience changed how you live?

- How has it changed your relationship with God?

Here are some more tips:

Always ask open-ended questions. Questions that can be answered "yes" or "no" will get you nowhere. Ask questions that allow the subject to expand and you to ask follow-up questions.

Never give your questions to your subject in advance; spontaneity produces better interviews than canned answers. And feel free to ask questions that aren't on your list of prepared questions.

Generally, you'll want to edit the interview so that the audience doesn't see or hear the interviewer. So before you begin, ask the subject to repeat each question back to you in his or her own words. For example, if asked, "Where did this happen?" the interviewee would respond, "This happened at home," not just, "At home."

Make sure to ask "feeling" questions. "How did you *feel* when that happened?" This gets beyond facts into the world of emotions.

Make sure your subject is comfortable. Remember that lights are warm and can get hot. Provide water, tissues, and a comfortable chair.

Sit so that your subject is facing you and simply talking to you. In a few minutes, especially if you banter back and forth for a little while, the person will forget about the cameras.

At the end of the interview, always invite the subject to add something that you might have missed in your questions.

Keep the cameras rolling even after you've told your subject the interview is over. As they relax, people often drop gems that can actually end up being the heart of the interview.

Here are a few basic interview questions to get you started...

- Tell me what happened.

- How did the experience affect your life or the lives of those around you?

- What did you learn from this experience?

- How has it changed you?

Filming and Editing

The filmmaker/editor is the key to ensuring that the visuals, sound, and pacing of the interview work together to support the big idea.

Here are a few tips for the person behind the camera and the person who will be editing the film:

- Use more than one camera. This gives you the ability to cut to a different vantage point, making the film more visually interesting.

- Take the time before the interview to get the lighting and sound right. Many a great story has been rendered unusable because of muddy sound or bad lighting.

- Capture more than head shots. Shoot the subject's hands, the back of his or her head, and so on. Again, this will make the interview more visually appealing and will provide cover for editing cuts.

- If possible, shoot some lifestyle footage of your subject. This footage can then be woven into the interview, fleshing it out and adding visual interest.

- Keep it short, short, short. It had better be a pretty compelling story to go over four minutes. We've found three and a half minutes to be perfect.

- When appropriate, use title cards to deliver an epilogue. (A title card is a piece of filmed, printed text edited into the video.) For example, at the end of an interview with a doctor who gives her time to repair cleft palates in developing countries, a title card might read, "In the past year, Dr. Kindness has given 39 children the confidence to smile." (And in this case, you could make the final frame a photo of a smiling kid who was helped by the doctor.)

Peer-to-Peer Interaction

Welcome to church!

Now grab a seat, and let us do all the heavy lifting! We'll be the water, and you'll be the sponge. We'll be the performers, and you'll be the audience. We'll be the professors, and you'll be the student.

Kind of typical, isn't it? And after all, most people don't come to church with a strong sense that they have anything to bring to the conversation or even that there's a conversation to be had.

And frankly, as a pastor, I'm a bit fearful of swinging open the gates and letting just anyone pontificate on whatever they want. We have more than a few bona fide nutcases who would jump at this opportunity and a whole lot of people so new to the gospel message that I'm not sure what they might say. In other words, I don't want the blind to lead—or stampede—the blind.

As a pastor, I'm a bit fearful of swinging open the gates and letting just anyone pontificate on whatever they want.

Better they just remain quiet and leave everything to the trained professionals.

Actually, no, it's *not* better.

Think about it. We are designed to *participate* in the world around us.

We take our kids to hands-on museums. Much of our electronic world is designed to broaden participation as we tweet, comment, respond, vote, like, and otherwise chime in. We share our photos, write our blogs, and watch and post homemade movies.

But when we enter the doors of a church, participation and interaction stop midway through the morning.

I propose that if the godly concepts being presented on Sunday morning are vital enough, people will want to respond to them in more than a passive way. They'll want to talk about them, give their feedback, and somehow feel that they're on a journey with those around them.

Giving people the chance to be part of the Sunday experience through more than their singing voices and monetary giving is part of what glues us together as a community.

I'll go a step further. What if the community experience sometimes included touching, tasting, smelling, and seeing as well as hearing and singing? Wouldn't those kinds of shared experiences bind us together more than inactive roosting and forced pleasantries during the "stand and greet someone you don't know" part of conventional services?

Of course, opportunities for peer-to-peer interaction must be carefully planned so that those frustrated preachers in the pews don't see this as an invitation to get on their soapboxes. But if the appropriate groundwork is laid at the outset, the boundaries you set will be respected.

Besides our own reluctance to let the lunatics run the asylum for a few minutes, in most churches the greatest barrier to any real peer-to-peer interaction is the seating structure. Pews put a damper on any kind of interaction that starts with "Turn to two or three people around you and talk about..." Ditto for auditorium seating and chairs that are clamped together. The ideal seating arrangement for this kind of activity is around 36-inch round tables, which frankly is a terrific but seldom-used idea.

But even if options for seating are limited, there are still plenty of ways to encourage peer-to-peer interaction.

Real-Time Polling

Because being asked to actually discuss something is a foreign concept in most congregations, you may have to start out slowly.

You could start with something simple, novel, and fun, such as a real-time poll.

This could be as simple as asking people to raise their hands in response to a question or two.

Or, by using cell phones, the congregation could respond anonymously to any yes-or-no or multiple-choice question you might ask. For example, you might ask, "What's your primary source of news and information: a newspaper, the radio, the Internet, or television?" Online polling allows you to show the results in graph form on the screen as they're punched into people's phones.

Or people can contribute their own ideas in a flurry of responses. For example, you could ask them to type in something they're thankful for, and the words would appear on the screen as they're being typed. (There are screening devices that allow someone to block out wacko responses—a very useful tool at a middle school camp.)

Imagine how the veterans in your congregation would feel if, on Veterans Day, everyone in the congregation honored them with a barrage of thanks that appeared on the screen in real time.

Polling gets everyone involved, gives everyone a voice (at least within a context), and encourages everyone to be honest. (So it may not be best to use a poll at the end of your message asking, "Isn't this the best sermon you've ever heard?")

This kind of polling service is easy to set up and inexpensive. (Check out polleverywhere.com.)

Polling isn't classic peer-to-peer interaction, but it does pave the way for actual dialogue, especially in congregations that may be hesitant to converse at first. We've certainly found that polling questions often spark deeper conversations or can be used in concert with conversations.

For example, in one poll we asked respondents to agree or disagree with this statement: "No culture is inherently better than another."

To our surprise, most people agreed with that statement.

We then put three photos on the screen: a Nazi rally from World War II, a photo of a tattooed gang flaunting their bad-boy poses for the camera, and a photo of ISIS soldiers lining up victims for execution.

After making a few comments, we asked the same question again, and the results were markedly different. We then asked everyone to turn to someone nearby and talk about the poll results. Then I moved into a message about the culture of the kingdom of heaven.

Straw Polling

Straw polls are another way to ease people into participation. For example, let's say you're delivering a message about sharing the faith and you want to show how many people in the world claim to be Christians and how many adhere to other major religions or claim no faith at all.

Well, these statistics are available online (one recent survey shows 31.5 percent Christian, 23.2 percent Muslim, 15 percent Hindu, 7.1 percent Buddhist, 16.3 percent nothing in particular, and 6 percent folk religions). Of course you could read the statistics or project them onto the screen. But to really make your point, you could do something like this:

Before Sunday, figure out your average attendance. For the purpose of this example, let's say it's 100 people. Round off the statistics above, then get colored cards to represent those figures—for instance, 32 blue, 23 green, 15 yellow, 7 white, 16 pink, and 6 purple. Shuffle the colors together, and, as people enter, distribute them at random along with the bulletin.

At the point in the message at which you would otherwise just state the statistics, ask all those with yellow cards to lift them up when you say, "Of the world's population, these are the Hindus." And so on. When all of the cards are being held up, everyone in the room will have a picture of the statistics that will stick with them a whole lot longer than a dry reading of the numbers ever could.

And congregants haven't had to do anything scarier than lift a card.

Answering Questions

Generally, when we ask people to interact with one another, we ask open-ended questions with no right or wrong answers. These questions usually allow people to respond from their experience. We avoid questions that give the biblically astute a chance to checkmate newbies who might give less than biblical answers.

Here are some examples of questions that prompt easy dialogue:

- Tell about a family tradition you grew up with.

- Tell about someone outside your family who influenced or encouraged you, and describe how.

- If you could talk with any historical figure other than Jesus, who would it be and why?

- If you were banished to a desert island and could take only one movie with you, what would it be and why?

While these questions are personal, they aren't intrusive.

When members of a congregation start to get used to interacting with one another, your questions can get deeper and more personal.

Peer-to-peer interaction can be a surprising twist when it's used at the end a message.

 Peer-to-peer interaction can be a surprising twist when it's used at the end a message.

For example, if the big idea is from James 1:27—that true religion is reflected in caring for widows and orphans, the most vulnerable in our society—close the morning with a five- to seven-minute discussion about the most vulnerable people in your neighborhood and how your church can care for them.

The questions might be framed like this:

- Who are the most vulnerable people in our community?

- What do they need care for, help with, or protection from?

- What are some practical things a group of believers could do to provide these things?

And here's an idea that always goes over well, especially if you're just beginning to give peer-to-peer interaction a try: Give everyone an ice cream bar to munch on while they talk. And tell them that when the ice cream is gone, that will be their cue to wrap up their conversations!

Some Caveats

I know some people are terribly uncomfortable sharing their thoughts with people they don't know well. Because it's critical that *everyone* feels comfortable, I always allow a way out by saying, "You can join a conversation as a listener if you aren't comfortable talking."

Also, be very aware of visitors and try to put them at ease. Most visitors are self-conscious anyway, so congregational participation might be particularly scary to them—especially since they probably haven't encountered it before. A simple way to help them relax is to let everyone know early on that you'll be giving them an opportunity to talk with each other at some point in the service.

I will often say something like this: "I know that most people come to church to hear someone like me be the fount of all knowledge, but we think you have something valuable to say and you might like to be part of the conversation. So at some point this morning, I'm going to turn it over to you for a few minutes, and I thought I'd give you fair warning. By the way, if you're new with us and this kind of thing is uncomfortable for you, that's okay. You can just listen in if you'd like."

Objects

Christians have used physical objects to make a point for a long, long time, but now the practice is generally restricted to children or youth because some feel it's too juvenile for adults.

I beg to differ…and I think Jesus does, too.

Apparently he didn't think using objects to make a point was beneath him or his audience. He used flowers, mud, coins, rocks, and other commonplace items to illustrate and anchor his teaching. And he used the common mealtime elements of his day to make a profound spiritual connection that resonates deeply with his followers to this day.

Holding up an object to illustrate a concept adds another dimension to the idea, and another dimension is added when people actually touch the object themselves (more on this later). The more dimensions, the better the retention.

A lot of people think that using objects is a gimmick. Okay, it *is* a gimmick, but if it gets an idea across better than mere words, I'll go with the gimmick every time.

It was just such a stunt that propelled me into ministry.

It was 1968. Candy bars cost a nickel, a bottle of soda a dime; anyone making $10,000 a year had an enviable career. And I was a poor kid, working for part-time wages of less than $3 an hour.

I was a member of a youth group. At one of the well-attended meetings, the leader stunned us all by pulling a $100 bill out of his wallet.

Most of us had never actually touched a hundred bucks in one piece of currency, so he passed it around so we could see it was genuine. As we were examining it, he talked about all the things a hundred bucks could buy at the time. (Think of this as a $1,000 bill in today's currency.)

Then he tossed out another shocker by saying that since this was *his* hundred bucks, while he had a plan for it, he might give it away to someone who could offer a good idea of how to spend it.

The room erupted as all of us offered competing plans for this huge resource. Most schemes, like mine, were about acquiring stuff (I would use it for a new surfboard), but some of the kids became benevolent, suggesting ways to give to the poor, while others got downright saintly and said they'd use it to fund missionaries or buy Bibles for people in countries where they were forbidden.

The youth leader smiled at the suggestions and commended some of the nobler ones. Finally, he got us all to pipe down so that he could drop this bomb: "You've given me some wonderful ideas of what I could do with this money. But it *is* my money, so I've decided to burn it."

We all thought he was joking until he pulled a book of matches out of his pocket and lit the bill on fire. When it was partially burned, he blew out the fire and explained that every life has potential for immense good and that all of us have the privilege of using our lives to do something meaningful or to waste them, to burn them up. Then he relit the $100 bill.

Kids begged him to stop, but he didn't. He ended his illustration by saying, "You might think I'm a fool for wasting so much money. But if even one of you decides to use your life differently because of this, it's worth it to me. It's money well spent."

And then he tossed the tiny corner of the $100 bill into the group of stunned kids.

I can't speak for anyone else in that room, but I got the point, and it's ingrained in me. I managed to retrieve the surviving corner of that burnt $100 bill and slipped it into my wallet. I've carried it ever since as a reminder of the moment that changed the arc of my life.

Objects don't have to be dramatic to do the trick. They can be simple, they can be clever, they can be big, and they can be small.

The main requirement is that they illustrate a spiritual concept or some part of a spiritual concept.

Not too long ago, I told a story to illustrate that we often carry useless junk that hinders us in our journeys. Hebrews 12:1 was the text: "Let us strip off every weight that slows us down" (New Living Translation).

The story was about a high-altitude backpacking trip I was part of. I had the bright idea to put a couple of cans of Dr Pepper (the nectar of the gods) into my pack to enjoy once we'd reached the summit.

The added weight was a burden that I carried to the top all by myself. When I popped the tab to enjoy the fruit of my labor, tin cups extended from the hands of my sad and hopeful companions, and I ended up getting just a few sips of the drink I'd struggled so long to carry. Conclusion: Like a lot of things we drag around with us, it wasn't worth the effort.

As I finished telling the story, the doors burst open, and in came a team of helpers with carts of Dr Pepper. Everyone was given a can along with a challenge: "For the next week, put this in your purse and take it with you to work, or put it in your backpack and take it to school. But you are *not* allowed to open it for a week. Let it remind you of the things of no real use that you carry around that just make your day harder."

Of course a few rebels opened their beverages in the parking lot (the cans were warm, so it served them right), but amazingly most people hauled those dumb cans around for a week. They sent us photos of the cans in their purses or on their desks and especially of them hoisting the soda can on the last day of the challenge.

Any object that illustrates a concept is better than no object at all because an object makes a visual connection to a spiritual, invisible idea.

Objects can also create interaction.

For example, in a teaching on 1 Corinthians 12, I wanted to convey the idea that the connectedness that comes from sharing lives in a local community of faith gives the world a much bigger picture of God than we can reflect by ourselves.

When people entered the room, they each found a piece from a puzzle on their chair. Then, based on their individual pieces of the puzzle, they were asked to guess what the picture was.

I then invited them to see if they could connect their pieces with the people around them and then to offer up a guess. This activity got everyone on their feet, trying out their puzzle pieces with those around them (which had been placed so that most pieces interlocked with the others in that section of the room).

This simple object put legs on an important idea and provided a way for people to interact with one another in a nonthreatening way.

I Touch, I Remember

One of the best ways to get people to remember a concept is to connect it with something they can touch. Whenever I can, I find a way for people to get their greasy mitts on an object related to the teaching. Nothing helps them cross the line from observers to participants as much as that sense of touch.

For example, we bought a few hundred small tools—screwdrivers, paintbrushes, tape measures, and so on—and, without explanation, handed them out at the door along with the bulletins one Sunday. (It sounds expensive, but I found a bunch of them on sale in packs and made good use of cheaper tools like carpenter pencils. It helped that I'd been planning this message for several months so I had time to collect the stuff.)

 We bought a few hundred small tools—screwdrivers, paintbrushes, tape measures, and so on—and, without explanation, handed them out at the door.

As they were handed a bulletin and a tool, people were befuddled, but when they asked the people at the door what they were for, they didn't know either, so everyone was equally befuddled.

At the end of our time together, they were no longer befuddled. They each carried with them a tangible reminder of some key biblical concepts: We're called to build up the body of Christ with the individual tools we've been given. And we all need each other to get the job done since no one tool can build a house.

Because they touched the tools and took them home, they'll remember the concept for a long, long time.

There's no magical way to always find the right thing to put in people's hands. Sometimes the object "has you" long before you realize how you might use it.

Once, while on vacation in a small town, I stumbled across a ramshackle shop that sold war memorabilia. I noticed a belt buckle for $30. It was of the kind worn by virtually every solider of the Third Reich. What caught my eye were the words that surrounded the Nazi eagle and swastika: "Gott Mit Uns," which, even with my limited German, I understood immediately. These soldiers—the rank and file working in offices or mess halls, those on the battlefield and those committing atrocities—all wore the same slogan: God is with us.

I bought that belt buckle long before I knew what to do with it. Eventually, I passed it around the congregation during a message warning of the foolishness of this world and the deceptiveness of sin. It was an electric, powerful way to amplify a biblical truth.

Here are a few more ideas for engaging people's sense of touch, possibly during a Good Friday or Easter service:

- Create a 3-D plywood cross, keeping the back open to make it lighter and easier to hang. Place the cross at the front of the meeting room. Break a number of different colored tiles into pieces, and put them in a basket near the cross. At an appropriate time during the service, cover the cross with tile mortar, and invite people to take a piece of broken tile, representing their brokenness, and press it onto the cross. The result is a beautiful mosaic representing broken believers.

- Place index cards and pens on chairs before the service begins, or pass them out as people enter. At some point in the service, invite people to write on a card the first letter of a sin or failing they're most ashamed of. Tell them they won't share this with anyone and to simply fold the card in half. Pass around baskets of spikes or large nails, asking people to drop their cards in and a take nail in exchange, illustrating the price Jesus paid for their forgiveness.

- Safely set up a small hibachi or some other burner in the meeting room. During the service, pass around a basket containing small tabs of incense, and ask everyone to take one. Invite people to respond to Jesus' sacrifice with prayers of gratitude. After the prayers, ask them to throw the incense into the burner in the spirit of Psalm 141:2, "May my prayer be set before you like incense." And yes, the church may smell like a Hindu temple, but because the sense of smell is the most evocative of all the senses, the connections made during this simple activity can be deeply memorable.

- Find a plant with long, nasty thorns, and fill a basket with clippings from it. Make a crown from a flexible material like dried grapevine. Place the basket next to the crown. At an appropriate point in the message, invite people to demonstrate their part in the event that sent Christ to the cross by picking up a thorny twig and placing it in the crown.

Anytime you can give people the chance to connect an intangible concept to a tangible object, you substantially increase their retention of the ideas you want to convey.

Music, Movies, and Other Media

I was devastated when they shot Old Yeller.

I know that only a few of you reading this have any idea of what I'm talking about, and those of you who do know also remember rotary phones and writing in cursive.

Old Yeller was the name of a dog in a Walt Disney movie by the same name. The dog was the star of the show in an era when Hollywood dogs such as Rin Tin Tin and Lassie were actually smarter than their owners.

Old Yeller had to be put down by the family that loved him because he went after a rabid wolf to save the life of his young master and, in doing so, contracted the disease.

I was just a 6-year-old kid, but the movie did a number on me. For the first time, I began to understand the concept of sacrifice.

Scenes from movies have moved all but cave dwellers and those with stone hearts. If certain scenes from *Schindler's List, Toy Story 3, Boy in the Striped Pajamas,* or *American Sniper* haven't choked you up, perhaps it's time to examine your pulse.

Because of film's immense power to inform, move, and inspire, why not grab short clips for use on Sunday?

BE SURE TO SEEK PROPER LICENSING WHEN USING SECULAR MUSIC OR VIDEO CLIPS. FOR MORE INFORMATION ABOUT LICENSING MUSIC, CHECK OUT CHRISTIANCOPYRIGHTSOLUTIONS. COM. FOR MOVIES, CHECK OUT CVLI.COM OR WINGCLIPS.COM.

For example, I used the end of *Saving Private Ryan* as a way to make the point of Colossians 1:10: "So that you may live a life worthy of the Lord and please him in every way: bearing fruit in every good work, growing in the knowledge of God."

In the film, Capt. John Miller and his squad have saved the life of Pvt. Ryan, but most of them have given their lives in the effort. As Miller lies dying, he implores the private to "earn" what he has been given. The next scene is of Ryan as an old man, standing in front of his captain's grave in Normandy, assuring him that he has tried to live a life worthy of Miller's sacrifice.

Connecting this scene with the Christian's reasons for living a worthwhile life is easy and very, very memorable.

Music can have a similar effect on our hearts and minds. Often a song can deliver a message in a far more compelling and memorable way than words alone ever could.

Want to comment on the importance of spending time with loved ones? Play the classic "Cat's in the Cradle" by Harry Chapin (yes, it's old, but it's truly timeless). In it, an aging father, who had neglected his boy as a child, now finds his grown son too busy to spend time with him because, he laments, "My boy was just like me."

Want a powerful addition to a message about the fact that there are times when almost everyone finds the idea of God very necessary? Play Regina Spektors' "Laughing With," which begins, "No one laughs at God in a hospital."

These are songs by secular artists; there are also tons of songs by believers (starting way back with the writers of the psalms) that convey messages in ways that really connect and stick.

And then there are other media.

You could use a whiteboard animation about an idea, word, or topic. Whiteboard animation mirrors an actual whiteboard and markers used in classrooms, but it's animated and can be sped up. (Think time-lapse photography.)

Several companies have developed programs that allow people with minor computer skills to create their own animation shorts complete with lip-sync. Check out GoAnimate.com or Sparkol. com. Both are subscription services that allow you to create your own videos.

Earlier I mentioned our Stories From the Red Chair and other videos our team creates. Your team can create your own videos and tap into the large and growing well of short videos created by others.

Check worshiphousemedia.com for a huge selection of videos. You can even find one we created here: worshiphousemedia.com/ mini-movies/50446/Unseen-Love.

A Continuing Conversation

One of my favorite things to do after a movie is to talk about the film with those who sat in the darkened theater with me. With the faint smell of buttered popcorn still on our fingers, we become movie critics as we examine the movie's theme, the motives of the characters, and the various questions prompted by the plot. Then when we get home, we recommend or "dis" the film to our friends on social media.

What if the Sunday morning service was not only an opportunity for worship but also a prelude to a series of continuing conversations? When the legions of churchgoers march off to their favorite post-church luncheon haunts, what if they were really chewing on concepts and questions arising from the big ideas presented that morning?

What if the Sunday morning service was not only an opportunity for worship but also a prelude to a series of continuing conversations?

Most pastors would be thrilled if their people spent the hour or so following the Sunday morning experience talking about the messages they've worked so hard to prepare. And while it's not possible to force this to take place, it's pretty easy to provide tools that invite that kind of conversation.

One great way to make that happen is to make sure your people have at least one *provocative* (think stimulating, challenging, incendiary) question placed in their hands before they leave the church premises.

What do I mean by *provocative*? Well, suppose the subject is stewardship, money, and contentment. Here are some thought-provoking questions that might lead to some spicy conversation:

- Most Americans say they don't necessarily want to be rich; they just want to be "comfortable." What would it take for you to be "comfortable"?

- How would you describe God's definition of "comfortable"? How would your lifestyle change if your comfort level were on a par with what God says we should be content with?

- Is there ever a point for Christians at which holding onto too much money is wrong? If so, what is that point, and why do you answer as you do?

- In light of the massive human need in this world, when, if ever, is it morally wrong to spend an exorbitant amount on a purchase? How do you know when you've crossed the line?

- Do you think God will hold us accountable for how we use our money? If so, in what sense?

Of course these questions don't have easy answers, and some may start a fight in the middle of the restaurant or even prompt people to change their orders to crackers and water, but it's their provocative, probing nature that makes the questions interesting and worth thinking about.

The easiest way to distribute conversation starters is to print them on cards and invite people to take one as they exit on Sunday morning. Or you can insert them in the bulletins.

While you're at it, encourage your people to post the questions on social media and invite their friends to respond to them.

And let your congregation know that you might be asking them about their discoveries. The following Sunday ask people what they talked about, and take a hand-held mic into the congregation to hear from those who want to share their answers. This is especially useful during a series, when you want to remind the congregation of the previous week's message as you transition to the next one.

You Figure It Out

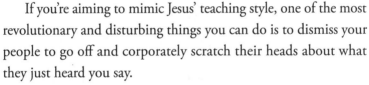

If you're aiming to mimic Jesus' teaching style, one of the most revolutionary and disturbing things you can do is to dismiss your people to go off and corporately scratch their heads about what they just heard you say.

Most of us who stand on a stage or behind a pulpit work hard to ensure that our messages are wrapped up nice and neat every week. We never want to take the chance that some people may not get the point we want them to get, because heaven forbid they should get the *wrong* point.

Apparently the Master had no such qualms.

Consider the words of Jesus on this subject:

"The disciples came up and asked, 'Why do you tell stories?' He replied, 'You've been given insight into God's kingdom. You know how it works. Not everybody has this gift, this insight; it hasn't been given to them. Whenever someone has a ready heart for this, the insights and understandings flow freely. But if there is no readiness, any trace of receptivity soon disappears. That's why I tell stories: to create readiness, to nudge the people toward receptive insight. In their present state they can stare till doomsday and not see it, listen till they're blue in the face and not get it'" (Matthew 13:10-15, *The Message*).

What if we created moments, told stories, or showed videos designed to stimulate thinking, questioning, debate, and discussion rather than always giving the answers? And what might this look like?

Well, for sure it would look like work for the people grappling with the unanswered questions. Often they'd rather have someone else do the hard work of discovery and then just tell them what to do.

To kick-start your thinking, here's a sample of what I'm talking about:

Suppose your message is about loving your neighbor. What if you ended it with a story like this?

> An empty house in your neighborhood has recently been rented to a single man.
>
> The man seems quiet, soft-spoken, and somewhat friendly, but he keeps to himself.
>
> One of your neighbors did some research on the Internet and found that he's a registered sex offender. As you can imagine, the word spread quickly, with predictable results.
>
> One Sunday, this man started coming to church... your church.
>
> Naturally, you think the pastor ought to know about this man's background. When you tell the pastor what you've discovered, he tells you that he's already met with the man, who told of his authentic conversion while in prison and his desire to serve Christ within the church in any way that would be helpful.

With all this in mind, how would you show love
to this man? How would you show love to those in
your neighborhood who fear this man? How would
you show love to your church family?

In some contexts, you could give people a few minutes to talk about this right then and there and then dismiss them. In other contexts, you could just lay out the dilemma and dismiss people to discuss it with their families and friends.

Here's another example:

One Sunday, after talking about opportunities to do good and bless others, I passed out a number of $50 bills at random. I assigned the recipients the task of using this blessing to bless others in return. Of course, I had some stipulations:

1. They had to identify a use for the money; they couldn't just give it back to a ministry.

2. They could spend the cash on themselves if they wished…but they might be asked to give an accounting of that blessing.

3. They could solicit ideas on how best to use the cash for God's glory, but they had to be the *primary actor* in distributing it.

4. No, they couldn't give it back, any more than people can give back their talents or opportunities.

These rules were designed to place the responsibility for figuring out how to bless others squarely on the shoulders of the individual.

We followed up, asking recipients what they did with the cash. And the following week, without naming names, we listed some of their choices: Some used the money anonymously to help a struggling friend or coworker. One paid camp fees for a student who couldn't afford to go.

Of course we didn't have to follow up. We could have just left it alone and let them report to us if they wished.

Intentionally failing to tie the bow on the Sunday morning package may annoy some people who feel it's the job of the pastor to not just ask questions but also to provide answers. But I would argue that sometimes the pastor's more important job is to provoke people to work out how to think and behave for themselves.

If you do this, I bet many of your people will thank you for the experience down the road.

What Do I Do With This? The "So What?" Factor

I feel a little dumb writing this section because I think it's sooooooo obvious. But having sat through countless sermons in which I had a bucket of theological ideas dumped on my head but nothing I could take home, I think it's a necessity.

The Sunday morning experience ought to do more than inform, entertain, or makes us feel good. It should *affect* us. It should give us ideas we want to act on. It should give us tools to *do* something, *change* something, *celebrate* something (or Someone), *fix* something, *aspire* to something, *attempt* something. At the very least, it should give us something to chew on.

The Sunday morning experience ought to do more than inform, entertain, or makes us feel good.

Now this is a tall order because those in attendance on any given Sunday are all over the board in their relationships with Christ, in their personal struggles or victories, in what plagues their thinking, as well as their age, their education, and their emotional responses to whatever they're dealing with when they walk in the door. One person may be highly affected by a message that others find only mildly engaging.

Over the years I've come to grips with the fact that it's impossible to connect with each individual in an equally impactful way from one Sunday to the next. But that doesn't mean we shouldn't give it our best shot.

Here are some things to consider as you grapple with the "So what?" factor:

Figure Out Who You're Aiming At

Who makes up your body of believers? Think about their ages, genders, and educational levels, as well as their spiritual states.

I've decided to make a 10th-grade boy the lowest common denominator for my messages. In other words, if a kid that age gets the big idea, can relate to the message, and can implement at least some of it, I've hit my mark.

But we have a lot of 10th-grade boys (or guys who think like 10th-grade boys) in our congregation. If our church were parked next to a place like Harvard, my lowest common denominator would surely be different. (Not sure if it would be higher or lower, but it would be different...)

Don't Get Too Nuanced

It takes an amazing communicator to inspire people of all ages, educational backgrounds, socioeconomic statuses, ethnicities, and levels of spiritual maturity. And I am not all that amazing.

As I was mulling over the question of how to even come close to hitting that goal, a question came to me: What seems to please pretty much everyone? And the answer was simple: an old-fashioned family meal.

When you think of a family meal, you probably don't think of gourmet food garnished with artsy doodads and served on dishes painted with some kind of food product.

You don't think of trying something new or exploring culinary delights from some obscure corner of the world. In fact, a family meal rarely features anything new at all, but it does have something for everyone.

Family meals connect with kids, adults, and teens. Family meals aren't a showcase for novelty or for mature palates. They're loaded with recognizable stuff that leaves everyone happy and full.

Like family meals, a lot of the best messages aren't brimming with gourmet theological nuances that no one has ever heard or considered. Most are just centered on familiar ideas that we need to be reminded of in fresh, compelling ways.

For example, who doesn't need to be reminded to encourage others or to cultivate gratitude toward God? Who doesn't need a nudge to recalibrate their thinking from earthly to heavenly? Who doesn't need to be reminded to take time to be still and seek God?

This is just what Jesus often did as he reminded those steeped in the Old Testament of the heart of their faith.

Who Says You Have to Use All of Your Time?

I'm not sure why, but most of us pastors seem to think we have to fill all the time allotted to us on Sunday mornings.

Once in a while the big idea can be presented so powerfully in a shorter period of time that the best thing to do is to say "amen" and tell folks to hang out and talk until the kids are released from their classes.

And I've been a pastor long enough to assure you that, while I've heard a lot of grumbling when a message goes long, I've yet to hear any complaints when it goes short.

Aim for Something Practical

For the most part, design the "So what?" part of the message to encourage a practical response.

For example, rather than concluding a message about thankfulness with an encouragement to be thankful, ask people to write the initials of several people who deserve written thank you notes and to commit to write and send them in the coming week. If God is the object of their thanks, encourage them to write out their thanks to him.

Special Ingredients

The ingredients I've described so far are the ones we commonly use. But sometimes we've stumbled upon extraordinary opportunities to make Sunday morning especially memorable.

For example, I once came across a former Broadway actor named Bruce Kuhn. He had committed the King James Version of the book of John to memory as well as *The Message's* version of the book of Acts. (Yes, I prostrated myself at his feet.)

I immediately looked for a way to integrate him into our services. One Sunday, I introduced him by saying simply, "And now, the Word of God." All he did for 30 minutes was to repeat, word-for-word, portions of the book of Acts. Now I know this may sound b-o-r-i-n-g, but it was, in fact, stupendous. Words on paper burst into life as if Luke were sitting at the dining room table talking to each and every one of us.

People were stunned, enthralled, completely captivated.

Bruce got a standing ovation.

Of course it isn't often that you can ask a Broadway actor to deliver the goods on Sunday morning, but it sure is fun when you can.

(By the way, if you're interested in inviting a professional actor to your church, here are a couple of leads: brucekuhn.com and curtcloninger.com.)

The point is, be on the lookout for *every* opportunity—from within your church and from beyond its doors—to bring the Word of God to life each and every Sunday morning.

PART

5

Get Your
Motor Runnin'

How to Introduce Experiential Worship

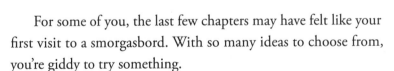

For some of you, the last few chapters may have felt like your first visit to a smorgasbord. With so many ideas to choose from, you're giddy to try something.

But I know that for others, as attractive as some of the ideas may be, and as much as you wish you could fold them into your Sunday services, you're well aware that any number of these ideas could spark an irate crowd scene straight from an old monster movie. Armed with torches, wooden stakes, and pitchforks, your people would clamor to end that which most churches fear more than false doctrine or a second offering: *change*.

The good news is that sweeping changes aren't necessary. There are ways to acclimatize the congregation and slowly introduce ways to make all your messages stick. If you're gentle, incremental, and wise, your congregation won't even realize that they're the "frog in the kettle."

 The good news is that sweeping changes aren't necessary.

So, to the tenuous, timid, or semi-adventurous, the next section is for you.

Easing Into the Shallow End

One of my former jobs was to teach preschoolers how to swim.

My dad thought the way to teach me was to toss me in over my head and let me get myself out of trouble, but most parents don't approve of that method. So I learned how to ease kids into the foreign world of liquid.

The kids came to me dry, so the first order of business was to get them wet. This was best accomplished by having everyone stomp around in ankle-deep water.

Stomping is natural to little kids, so pretty soon everyone was wet from head to toe but didn't care. (And yes, I played, too, aiming some stomps so that they'd drench kids who were hesitant to get with the program.)

The next step was to descend slowly into the pool, one step at a time. This usually took a few sessions as well as a few gimmicks. ("Oh, no! We've all been turned into turtles! And turtles have to be in the water, or they'll die! Quick! All turtles into the water!")

Of course, the highest hurdle was getting kids to put their faces in the water. I started by having everyone blow bubbles. Eventually I dropped my locker room keys in a spot that required the kids to get their mugs underwater in order to retrieve them so that we could all get to our towels.

All of this didn't happen in one day, but in the end nearly all of the kids were comfortable in a world they'd feared when we started.

The same kind of techniques are helpful for exposing folks to a new paradigm when many are quite content with the old one.

As we all know, many people—especially church "lifers"—are picky about what happens in a worship service. Some get white-hot mad if you don't say, "Turn in your Bibles to…" even though the text is being projected on the screen (because, I assume, people in the early church always carried their Bibles with them to Sunday meetings).

Some people are married to a style of preaching or teaching. Some to verse-by-verse exposition, some to cleverly titled series such as "What's Up, Doc?" (about the Ascension) or "Is God Your Steering Wheel or Your Spare Tire?" For some, a sermon must have at least three points (preferably containing plenty of alliteration: "The Pugnacious Peter," "The Perplexed Peter," and "The Proclaiming Peter," for example).

So the first thing is to recognize that you can't please everyone… and that's okay.

Really.

The first thing is to recognize that you can't please everyone...and that's okay. Really.

Yet there is wisdom in wading in slowly so that you don't freak out everyone, and, if necessary, fooling them a bit—for their own good, of course. So here's a guide for s-l-o-w-l-y introducing the ideas in this book to your less-than-flexible congregation.

Generally young adults will offer much less resistance to change, so this advice is slanted toward those who have logged a lot of hours in the pews.

Start With Stories

People love a good story, and most good communicators are naturally good storytellers. A good story puts flesh on an idea, connects people with one another, and leaves a lasting impression.

Use Photos and Illustrations

This, of course, assumes that your church has entered the new millennium and has traded in the overhead projector and cassette deck for a video projector and computer. (Don't laugh...your church may still have those antiques in a closet somewhere, "just in case.")

Photos and illustrations work especially well if they're clever or funny. And, naturally, they must support your message. Even if to simply clarify an idea, an image enhances a message. For example, if you're talking about the parable of the wedding party that ran out of lamp oil, help to make the message stick by showing a photo of an ancient olive oil lamp.

The key is to make sure the photo or illustration appears on screen at the right time. If you speak from an outline, give your multimedia person a copy with the cue for the photo underlined or printed in red.

Use Video Testimonies

For those under 40, *testimony* is the old church term for "faith story."

Most church people are used to the idea of people telling their stories, so throwing up a testimonial video, especially if it showcases someone they know, always engages them. And video allows you to keep the story tight and concise.

But the story doesn't have to be about someone in the congregation. Sometimes you can go online and find short videos of famous people telling their faith stories, and they can be used to great effect.

This teaching device is easy to use and doesn't freak out a stiff congregation. If you haven't hired a storyteller and need someone to help you edit videos, ask an eighth-grader for help.

Use Simple, Nonthreatening Polling

Polling gets people used to participating in some way other than merely sitting and listening. It allows them to have input into a part of the message.

And there are lots of ways to poll people without making them uncomfortable. For example, if your text is about bringing kids to Christ, you could begin your message with this simple poll:

Ask everyone to stand. Then ask all those who became believers when they were children to turn around and face the back of the meeting room, those who became believers as teenagers to turn to their right, and those whose faith journeys started after they were 18 or who are still working it out to continue facing the front.

You'll end up with a lot of people facing different directions, but probably a significant number will be facing the rear or sideways, which will give you a visual segue into the message or a memorable affirmation of the message.

Use Objects

Objects don't have to involve fire or explosives to be effective. Simply producing an object tied to the message piques curiosity and improves retention.

Talking about fruit of the Spirit? Load up a bowl with a wide variety of delicious fruits and refer to them throughout the message. If you have the courage, wrap it up by walking into the congregation and handing out the fruit.

Talking about bearing each other's burdens? Bring a stretcher up front, and discuss the idea that sometimes we carry and sometimes we must be carried.

Use Special Events to Introduce More Adventurous Methods

The typical church calendar is full of opportunities to step away from the "same place, same thing" way of delivering a message and to explore new methods without making the troops crazy.

Christmas Eve services offer a great opportunity to tell the Nativity story creatively.

Instead of printing a typical bulletin, create a mini newspaper telling the gospel story, and print it on newsprint. Ask some young teens to dress as 1920s newsboys, and put them to work hawking the "Good news!" at the entrance of the building. This way, the bulletin, which is usually disposed of almost immediately, becomes a keeper to take home and read again.

Easter services are a great time to experiment with tag-team teaching. Divide the message into the Bad News (our sin, Jesus' death on the cross) and the Good News (the Resurrection). Have two gifted teachers share short teaching duties buffered by worship music, video clips, and so on.

Moving Toward the Deep End

This section is for you few brave souls who are ready to throw caution to the wind and try things that few others have.

Bear in mind that you'll need to have your leaders with you if you move in this direction, and even then, it will be important to ease your congregation into these waters.

If you're starting a new work, this new teaching style could be the hallmark of your church and set you apart from the cookie-cutter style used in other churches.

So pull up your big-kid britches, and off we go!

Go With Café Tables

If at all practical, use 36-inch round café tables, and have the congregation sit in groups of four around them. It may strike you as shocking, but the results are terrific.

I first saw this in practice years ago in an alternative worship service at a Presbyterian church in Southern California. Jeannie McCoy, the church's worship leader, cooked up the idea, and it was a marked and welcomed difference from the formal worship service that was offered at the same hour in the sanctuary.

The format helped retain a good number of people who were tired of attending without connecting and had been on their way out the door.

Café tables immediately relay the message that this isn't going to be the same old church experience. They encourage a much wider range of interaction as well as a handy place to park the coffee cup.

One ministry that has fully embraced this model is Lifetree Café. While it's not a church per se, the hour-long conversations that take place there every week could very well develop into one. Check out LifetreeCafe.com.

Make Peer-to-Peer Interaction Part of the Service

Whether it's early in the service, in the middle of the message, at the end, or during the drive home, make discussion an integral part of the Sunday experience.

Craft your questions carefully, making sure they're open-ended, surprising, specific, personal, and always, always relevant to the big idea of the message.

For example, if you're talking about the parable of the prodigal son, here's a great discussion question to ask right out of the gate: "You have plenty of money. Your children, aged 25 and 27, ask you for their inheritance now. What do you do?"

Here are a couple of other examples of provocative questions: "An armored car crashes in front of you, and $100 bills are floating across the highway. People are stopping to scoop them up, cramming them into their pockets. What would you do?"

"A waiter is working in a restaurant where tips are pooled. He's been given a lottery ticket as a tip, and he slips it into his pocket. It turns out to be a winner, and he's now a million bucks richer. Should he share the money with his co-workers?"

For more provocative moral questions like these, check out the game Scruples.

Embrace Open Endings

From time to time, tell an open-ended story or present a dilemma to the congregation. Again, be sure that the question applies to the morning's message. Create extra buzz by encouraging people to post their responses on social media.

For example, after a message on 1 Peter 2:21, 23 and 3:15-17 about how to respond to unbelievers, you might pose this situation:

Your brother has a son whose biology teacher is an atheist. The teacher loves to ridicule the intelligence of anyone who believes in God. Many of the kids think his rants are hilarious and enjoy hearing him bash those who think humans were created rather than evolved.

The teacher doesn't know your nephew is a believer, and the boy has kept his mouth shut so far, but his patience with the teacher's outbursts is wearing thin.

What advice would you give to the boy?

Handling Skeptics

The ideas in this book will cause the skeptics in your church to wring their hands at the prospect of failure. They'll throw a wet blanket on every idea and predict that no one will participate. They might even declare that people will leave the church in droves.

And these are the encouraging ones.

While it may not be possible to silence all the skeptics, it is possible to win a number of them over or at least convince them to give some of these ideas a try.

Do Your Prep

Before altering even slightly the way you currently do things, begin to break ground and sow the seeds of new ideas by having "What if?" discussions with people you know to be influencers.

Send them articles and examples of interactive and experiential teaching methods, asking them for their comments.

Take key leaders out for coffee to share some of your ideas. Ask them to partner with you in making these changes. Find ways to involve them in your scheme, especially the ones you envision as part of the team that will help you create Sunday experiences. Let them know that this is an experiment and that you'd like them to help you evaluate what worked and what didn't after each service.

 Take key leaders out for coffee to share some of your ideas. Let them know that this is an experiment.

It may be best to tell those who are especially resistant to change that you're seeking ways to make the Sunday experience more impactful and simply ask them to support you in prayer. This will give them a sense of ownership when you begin to roll out new ways of doing things.

The idea is to create a partnership with as many people as you can, especially influential ones, way before you introduce new methods into the service.

What you absolutely do not want to do is suddenly flip the switch from passive observation to full interaction and involvement. The shock of such a sudden shift may be more than your congregation can bear.

Demonstrate the Value of Change

Jeff was a kid in my middle school group when I was a youth pastor. He was one of my "lab rats" when I began experimenting with experiential learning.

Each week I would involve the kids deeply in some kind of hands-on activity that illustrated a teaching from the Bible. We had only two rules: First, everyone had to participate. Second, no one could do anything that hindered someone else's understanding.

Sometimes Jeff wasn't into it, but that didn't excuse him from participating. Once, during a drama dealing with a teaching from the Sermon on the Mount, Jeff didn't want a speaking part, so he was cast as the rock that Jesus sat on.

One morning before we began, Jeff approached me with a complaint.

"Can you tell me why we always have to do dumb stuff on Sunday morning? You make us draw, write stories, act out skits, and junk like that!" he groused.

"Well, Jeff," I said brightly, "I have you doing this kind of dumb stuff because it helps you learn."

His looked puzzled.

"Okay, Jeff, let me show you," I said. "What did you do here last week?"

"I made a newspaper article about Jesus walking on the water," he responded.

"And what was the message of that?" I asked.

"Um, I think it was that God is in control, so no matter what's happening around us, he has us covered."

Then I asked if he could remember what we did the week before.

He could. "I made a feractory or something," he said.

"Yes, you made a *phylactery*," I said. "And what was that about?"

"It was about making sure God's Word gets inside you, not just outside you," he replied.

"Bingo!" I said with two thumbs up.

Jeff managed to remember eight lessons in a row, even the one in which he played a rock. He remembered all eight experiences and the meaning behind each of them before his memory fuzzed out.

"So, Jeff, you just came from the first church service, right?"

"Yeah."

"And you listened to the pastor's message?" (The pastor was a very good communicator, by the way.)

"Uh-huh," Jeff mumbled.

"Well, can you tell me what it was about?"

Jeff's eyes went blank. I could tell he was searching every memory chip in the cranium, but he was coming up empty.

After a second, he said, "I dunno. I can't remember."

"Yep!" I said, "Which is *exactly* why we do all these dumb things each Sunday morning."

And from that Sunday on, I never got another complaint from Jeff. The results of the dumb stuff were self-evident.

In preparing this book, I mentioned some of what I was explaining in these pages to our church's office manager. She promptly started recalling the most memorable...uh, er, stunts, that took place during past messages that had caused a sea change in her spiritual life.

"Do you remember when you gave everybody a bag of potato chips?" she asked.

Reading the vague look in my eyes, she said, "Oh, it was years ago. It was a message about having a thirst for God, and you passed out salty chips. You encouraged us to eat the chips while you explained the passage, which made everyone so thirsty that we were all suffering."

I remembered. "Oh, yeah...and then at the end, I had the ushers give everyone a bottle of water."

"Yeah!" she said. "I always remember that illustration when I think about my desire for God."

It's these kinds of anecdotal examples that will demonstrate the value of the changes you're making. Keep a record of them, and share them.

The Tough Nuts

Some people are in love with the idea of preaching. I don't mean preaching in the sense of the official definition, which means "to proclaim." I mean preaching in the sense of an oral monologue expounding on Scripture.

Historically this *manner* of proclamation was not only popular, but for years it was the only show in town. However, not everything that once worked well in the preaching department still does.

At certain points in history, a man on a street corner or in a marketplace proclaiming the message of Christ would have drawn a crowd. Today he would cause people to quicken their pace and avert their eyes. Nothing wrong with the message, but the medium isn't connecting.

At certain points in history, titling a Sunday message "A Divine and Supernatural Light: Immediately Imparted to the Soul by the Spirit of God, Shown to Be Both a Scriptural and Rational Doctrine" wouldn't have sent people running for the hills. (Try getting that on your church sign.) It would have seemed normal.

And yes, that famous sermon by Jonathan Edwards was as long as the title suggests. You can read it online, but please don't try to preach it on Sunday unless you give everyone some NoDoz first. It's full of good stuff, but it would go down with a thud today.

Even so, some people plant their flag on the hill of a particular model of preaching and won't countenance any other, even if it works better.

These are the tough nuts to crack—and to be honest, you may never be able to crack them if you want to explore new methods of teaching.

Bill Easum, a man with a long history of helping churches grow, is famous for saying, "What keeps a church from growing usually comes down to one or two people." These would be the tough nuts, the folks so committed to their favorite styles or ways of doing things that they torpedo any other concepts.

So in some cases, no matter how much you may explain or reason, there may be people who will fight you every step of the way.

And it means that, to succeed, you'll have to be willing to see them go.

In Real Time: An Example of How It Happens

Theory is one thing; turning that theory into a workable proposition is another thing altogether. So I invite you to come along as I describe the process of turning some of the ideas you've been reading about into a message—a message our team delivered just last Sunday, in fact.

Of course, my church is different from yours, so as you read, imagine what tweaks you would make to implement this kind of teaching style in your church's unique context.

But first, let me tell you a few things about our congregation.

A Snapshot of Kauai Christian Fellowship

In many respects, we're an unusual church. Probably a quarter to a third of the people who show up are visitors, and most of them are visiting for the first time. Crazy, huh?

This is because the church happens to be half a mile from the largest visitor destination on the island of Kauai. The island has a population of 67,000, and there are many small but long-established churches on it. At nearly 25 years old, we're the relatively new kids on the block.

Like many newer churches, we started in a rented building and quickly outgrew our facilities. We were blessed to find six acres of land near the beach at a bargain price and built a new campus there.

When we opened the doors for the first time, the entire staff was astonished at how many visitors showed up. We'd thought most Christians on vacation would skip church; after all, that's what most of *us* would do. Nope. These visitors to Hawaii turned out to be a lot more spiritual than we are.

 When we opened the doors for the first time, the entire staff was astonished at how many visitors showed up.

This influx of visitors presents unique challenges each week. They come from a variety of faith backgrounds and traditions and enter a church where they have no friends, no history, and no idea of what they're in for.

Well, that's not exactly true. A surprising number of these visitors check us out on our website first.

Initially we were caught off guard and had to rethink how this dynamic might affect what we do on Sunday. After all, we want these visitors from all over the world to feel at home, and we want to make it easy for them to join in.

We offer a laid-back, contemporary worship service. Most of the band is barefoot and sports loose aloha shirts. Our worship leader realized it would be important to include one or two worship songs or amped-up hymns that are likely to be familiar to nearly everyone. We figured (correctly) that without these common tunes, many visitors would simply remain quiet throughout our time together.

With so many off-island visitors, we also realized it would be hard for our local folks to make solid connections with one another, so we concentrated on creating a vibrant small group ministry to help create community.

Our growth has been slow and steady. We're not a mega-church by mainland standards, but with at least 500 people attending two services, we're now the largest church on the island. And unlike most churches on the mainland, our 8:30 a.m. service is packed. It seems that people in Hawaii like to get a head start on Sunday morning.

So that's our church. It's unique in many ways, but it probably has more in common with the average church than it has differences.

With that background, come along and peer over my shoulder as our team develops and delivers a message.

Getting Started

Like many pastors, I'm currently working on a series. It's called "The Monkey Wrench of God," and its premise is that we human beings are prone to creating our own designs for living that God knows won't serve us well. So in his perfect love, he often tosses a monkey wrench into our systems and assumptions in order to get us to do things his way.

Simple.

I listed 10 or 12 areas—such as money, culture, and relationships—where God might toss a monkey wrench into our way of doing things.

Last week the message centered on our desire for privacy.

We decided to focus on three areas that people tend to keep private but God may not want to be private: our faith, our possessions, and our struggles. Our goal was to move people toward becoming transparent believers who travel light through life.

The Sunday Morning Outline

With that in mind, we decided on this flow:

- **Two Opening Songs**—All the songs chosen for this message were selected with an eye to our overarching theme.

- **Three-Minute Teaching**—The worship leader introduced the next song by drawing attention to a verse in the song that conveys the idea that becoming transparent is part of a Christ-follower's journey. In so doing, he set up an idea we would revisit at the end of the message.

- **Song Connected to the Message's Point**—The lyrics of this song affirmed the worship leader's short commentary.

- **Object 1**—An actual monkey wrench was tossed onto the stage, making a loud clunk. I picked it up and held it as I introduced the topic. (I keep wanting to come up with a piece of machinery that I could drop the monkey wrench into, causing smoke and sparks; alas, I don't have the budget or the stage hands for that kind of gimmick.)

The monkey wrench gives a quick picture of the overarching concept, and I've used it in the three previous messages in this series. As the series progresses, I'm starting to hear people in the congregation use the term *monkey wrench* when God allows their plans to go awry.

- **Peer-to-Peer Interaction**—Because we have so many visitors, I set up peer-to-peer interactions by explaining that we don't believe it's good for the pastor to do all the work on Sunday morning while everyone else sits and watches, so we ask for help with some of the heavy lifting. Then I invited people to turn to someone they didn't come with and share their answers to the following question, which was projected on the screen:

> Which of these questions do you think the average person would be the most *uncomfortable* with?
>
> 1. How much do you make?
>
> 2. Have you ever been arrested?
>
> 3. When was the last time you cheated?
>
> 4. What percentage of your income do you give to the Lord's work or charity?

Because there's no right or wrong answer to this question, it really got people buzzing. In fact, it took some effort to get them quieted down after the allotted discussion time.

(By the way, depending on the nature of the questions, we usually allow two to four minutes for people to respond.)

This peer-to-peer interaction made it easy to introduce the topic. I said something like this: "Most people would rather keep some areas of their lives private, and it's exactly in those areas where the monkey wrench of God will land. We'll explore three of those areas."

- **Object 2: A Private Faith?**—For this part of the message, I pulled out a small wooden box containing a photo-sized depiction of Jesus.

  I explained that we live in a world where we are expected to keep our faith private, to keep Jesus in a little box and never, ever bring him out, except at home. (About half of the people on debate.org say that people should keep their religious beliefs to themselves.)

  And, I suggested, this is where the clear teaching of the New Testament (1 Peter 3:15 and Matthew 28:19) throws a monkey wrench into the idea of a private faith.

- **Peer-to-Peer Interaction**—The second concept we wanted to cement is that private ownership is not a particularly Christian idea. We began by posing these questions on the screen:

What's the difference between being a steward and being an owner?

How do the responsibilities, attitudes, and emotions of a steward differ from those of an owner?

Once again, we asked people to turn to someone nearby and respond to these questions. And, again, much buzzing ensued.

- **Scripture**—Then I used modern language to tell the story from Luke 19:29-31 about the colt Jesus told his followers to "borrow" on Palm Sunday. Remember, Jesus told his followers that if anyone were to ask why they were taking the colt, they were to simply say, "The Lord needs it." (In telling the story in the modern vernacular, the colt became a Nissan Versa, making the story easier for our listeners to relate to.)

  So of course the question for our congregation was "What does the Lord have need of in your 'private collection'? Your stuff? Your talents? Your time? Your creativity?"

- **Story**—To set up the third idea—that people tend to keep their struggles private—I told an old Greek fable. It's kind of creepy, but it was no doubt familiar to every kid during the time of Christ. It's called "The Spartan Boy and the Fox," and it goes like this:

  > Once there was a young Spartan boy, who, like all Spartans, was taught from childhood to never show pain and to tough out in silence even the most distressing thing.
  >
  > On his way to school one day, the young man came upon a cage of small foxes whose owner was not around. Deciding he wanted one for himself, he stole one and hid it in his robe.
  >
  > He arrived at school, and, clutching the wiggling fox to his breast, he sat in class, trying to listen to his teacher.
  >
  > But the fox wanted out, so the boy, afraid that his theft would be discovered, clutched the beast even tighter.
  >
  > So the fox began to claw at the boy.

> Of course this caused him great discomfort and pain, but being a Spartan, he sucked it up and pulled the fox even closer.
>
> The pain worsened as the fox dug deeper, but still the boy wouldn't let him go. Then suddenly the young Spartan turned pale and collapsed as the fox escaped from his robe.
>
> His astonished classmates discovered that the boy was dead. The fox, which he had tried so hard to hide, has clawed into his heart.

(I know, I know. It's not the kind of story you'd tell your 5-year-old, but then again neither are the original Grimms' Fairy Tales.)

I then tied the story to James 5:16: "Therefore confess your sins to each other and pray for each other so that you may be healed."

- **Video**—Our storyteller shot and edited a story we titled "The Transparent Man," and we used it to wrap up the message.

  It's the story of a member of our congregation named Aaron. At various points in his life, Aaron has been involved in all kinds of activities that are seldom acknowledged, including drugs, theft, prostitution, porn, and adultery. Aaron has learned to be upfront with his struggles to the point of complete transparency. In the video, he talked about the freedom that's come with his ability to talk to trusted brothers about any temptation he faces.

  This closing—which encouraged people to be open about their failings and struggles and was delivered by a member of our own congregation—made the point in a far more powerful way than I ever could.

Later in the week, Aaron told me that he'd been fielding calls from people left and right, thanking him for his openness and for encouraging them to follow his example.

Oh…did I mention that at the end of the video, the congregation broke out in spontaneous applause?

- **Two Worship Songs and the Offering**

- **Closing Worship Song**

And There You Have It

That was a quick sketch of one Sunday's message.

What will next Sunday's message loo k like? Well, I can't tell you exactly. We may have music threading through the whole morning, we may use two or three teachers, we might have a panel on stage, or we could ask three questions of three different people. I don't know, but I'm meeting with my team soon and can give you a better idea then.

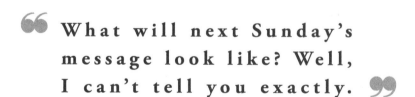

What will next Sunday's message look like? Well, I can't tell you exactly.

A Note of Encouragement

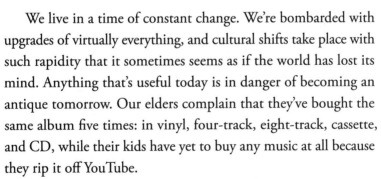

We live in a time of constant change. We're bombarded with upgrades of virtually everything, and cultural shifts take place with such rapidity that it sometimes seems as if the world has lost its mind. Anything that's useful today is in danger of becoming an antique tomorrow. Our elders complain that they've bought the same album five times: in vinyl, four-track, eight-track, cassette, and CD, while their kids have yet to buy any music at all because they rip it off YouTube.

In times such as these, it's tempting to view the contents of this work as just another fad that will quickly be replaced by another trend.

And to be honest, I don't know what new technology is around the corner. Will I someday give a message in a studio and simply have my hologram join the members of the congregation, who no longer meet in mass but in small clusters in living rooms?

Or will some solar hiccup cause all the satellites to come crashing down, forcing everything to go in reverse?

The possibilities are endless, but I do know this: No matter what tools we have at our disposal, all people, at all times, will hunger to be connected with God and with their fellow human beings.

Providing a space for those connections is what the church is all about.

The methods, tactics, and gimmicks described in these pages are all in pursuit of that goal. So please take whatever ideas are useful and put them to work. Do what you can to deepen and strengthen your people's connections to their Master and each other.

And if you come up with a brilliant way to do this, please share it. Some of us would be more than happy to borrow it.

HERE'S A FRESH TAKE ON SERMONS THAT WILL CATCH THE EAR OF A NEW GENERATION OF CHURCHGOERS

Readers discover how to connect with an audience that...

- Consumes sound bites, not sermons
- Processes information visually, not verbally
- Applies concepts through experiences and interaction, not lecture

Sermons Reimagined leads you through what it takes to not just capture that audience, but to captivate it— and keep it coming back Sunday after Sunday.

ISBN 978-1-4707-1670-7

$14.99 (U.S.)

Available at group.com or a Christian bookstore near you.

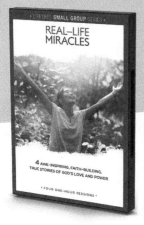  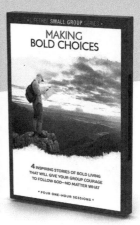